Personality in Handwriting

By the same author

GRAPHOLOGY FOR EVERYMAN

THE GRAPHOLOGIST'S ALPHABET

A HANDWRITING QUIZ BOOK
  (*Published by Gerald Duckworth & Co. Ltd.*)

HANDWRITING AND MARRIAGE
  (*Published by Rider & Co.*)

Personality in Handwriting

THE GUIDING IMAGE IN GRAPHOLOGY

by

ERIC SINGER

Illustrations by Gertrude Elias

DUCKWORTH

SECOND IMPRESSION 1974
FIRST PUBLISHED 1954

Cloth ISBN 0 7156 0786 3
Paper ISBN 0 7156 0785 5

Printed in Great Britain
by Unwin Brothers Limited
The Gresham Press, Old Woking, Surrey
A member of the Staples Printing Group

CONTENTS

v

INTRODUCTION

GRAPHOLOGY, now read as a subject at seven—and probably more—German universities, has made enormous progress all over the world and has become a complex science in its own right.

Everybody who has read my introductory books *Graphology for Everyman* and *The Graphologist's Alphabet* (of which the second should be read again, together with this book) will know that there are many aspects of graphology; they include the study of the guiding image and the dynamics of the executing movement, the development of the technique of analysis, and the application of the science to different practical purposes. Finally, there is the history of the science.

Of all these, the guiding image is one of the oldest parts of theoretical investigation. But oddly enough—while there are many comprehensive studies on the dynamics of the executing movement, producing the actual writing motion—a complete, comprehensive and, at the same time, exclusively theoretical and systematically elaborated system of the eidetic side of graphology, a handbook on the image in writing, is up to now lacking, though almost all sides of it have been elaborately and brilliantly investigated in different works.

This work attempts to fill this gap. I hope that it will not only be welcome to serious students of the science and, of course, to all my readers, to the Press and to everybody who, up to now, has encouraged my efforts, but that it will also help to convince wider circles and will bring nearer the day of general official and universal recognition of graphology in this country.

I wish to thank the editor of the London evening paper *The Star* for permission to use some of the illustrations published therein in connection with a series of articles by me which first appeared there.

Introduction

I also want to express my sincere gratitude to all my friends in the teaching profession who by furnishing me with writing examples and information have made my investigations possible.

Eric Singer

29 Abercorn Place, London, N.W.8
February 1954

CHAPTER I

LEARNING HOW TO WRITE

To discuss the psychology of writing and the learning of it means being involved with the controversial views of different psychological schools like association-psychology and *Gestalt*-psychology, also different schools of teaching of handwriting. We can, however, accept as common ground that writing has to be learned and can only be achieved by learning, but that there are different stages in the training and development, until a person reaches his individual standard of writing maturity, which means that the writing process becomes as automatic as this particular person is able to achieve it.

The first stage on the way to the learning of writing is the learning of speech. The child absorbs the sound of words, remembers them, forms sound images of words which it learns to connect automatically with certain recurring perceptions of forms and movements. To achieve that, it practises by imitation, trial and error, the movement of lips, tongue and larynx, enabling it to produce these sound images in an articulate and intelligible way. These movements and the particular achievements are individually conditioned by the particular character of the individual instruments of perception, execution and control of language (hearing, larynx, lips, mouth), all of which differ. Individuals differ also in the particular character of motor impulses stimulating the utterance of speech (quick, slow, fluent, interrupted, strong, weak, rhythmic, arrhythmic, etc.). Speech is also conditioned by different individuals' different wealth of observed sounds and imitated patterns.

As the child practises the movements of speaking, it adapts them to its own means of speech and will finally concentrate on the various modes of movements which are most congenial, easy and pleasant to it. These particular movements it will repeat until they become completely automatic; in this way the child will add

9

movement images to the sound images and perception images until the three become completely united and automatic.

Whether all this development is more or less of a simultaneous nature, as the *Gestalt*-psychologists contend, is a matter of opinion, but the result is in any case that the movement pictures which produce the sounds are automatically remembered and brought into action when the person is stimulated to speak either by perception or by thinking. The child sees its father, or thinks of its father, and automatically remembers the sound image which produces the word "father", and this enables it to say "father". In this way the elements of speaking (utterance, reference and evocation) become one simultaneous act.

The process of learning to write is of a somewhat similar nature. It differs from learning to speak, however, in many respects, chiefly in the following:

(1) While learning to speak begins with the learning of sound pictures of whole words, learning to write by present methods is effected by the learning of little pictures of the single letters of the alphabet.

(2) While the executive body instruments of speaking are the larynx, tongue and lips, the executing body instruments of writing are the arms, the hands, the fingers. In addition some external technical instrument for execution and preservation (writing instruments—pen, pencil, ink, paper) is necessary.

(3) While the main sense of perception and control in speaking is the sense of hearing, for writing it is the sense of sight. Speaking is controlled by the ear, while writing is controlled by the eye and by the sense of touch.

(4) While speaking does not fix or preserve its movements, the writer's manuscript is the fixation of his writing movement on the paper.

(5) The fact that the writing is manual work and requires an instrument creates different forms of resistance to its achievement.

(6) While the purpose of speaking is normally more or less always evocative, the purpose of writing is sometimes only to preserve some thoughts (notes, copying).

(7) Learning to speak is more or less left to chance, while learning to write is organized and synchronized with learning to read.

(8) (This difference is important to the graphologist.) The fact that writing is the imitation of a standard form and fixed and preserved on paper enables us to study and to compare it and to assess an individual's deviations from the standard of the copybook form.

If we want to analyse the sources of these deviations, we have to divide the process of the acquisition of the individual style of writing into elements:

(1) The copybook form imitated as standard.

(2) The writer's individual conception of the picture he wants to produce, the *guiding image*. This guiding image is a mark of the writer's individual taste. It is the complex sum of forms which he likes, and therefore remembers and imitates. It also indicates what forms he dislikes, wishes to forget and therefore excludes from his writing. The further question, how these likes and dislikes originate in each individual writer, penetrates to the very core of personality. One factor in choosing these particular images will be the individual perception apparatus of the writer. Another will be connected with pleasant or unpleasant memories; but the most important revelation of these deviations and individual forms is that they disclose the writer's individual experience of space. "The most personal thing", thought eighty-year-old Freud—as the last entry before his death in his *London Notebook* reveals—"is the individual's experience of space." His rival pupil Adler based his whole system on the personal experience of distance.

(3) The writer's ability to learn and remember automatically and to execute the necessary movement pictures. Here is involved not only the intelligence, the memory, the speed, rhythm and coordination of movements and the strength of motor impulses; the tracing itself requires the concentration of the elementary rhythm of whole body movements on the single movement required. There may be a hard struggle between opposed impulses, full of mutual compromises and many little tricks which reveal a great deal about the writer's methods of adapting his personal rhythm of movement, his physical powers to a special purpose dictated by will or outside circumstances. It is especially interesting to follow this struggle in children's handwritings as examples 1 to 6 show.

(4) The speed of his writing reveals the writer's own sense of speed and of time.

(5) Accidental sources of deviation, such as external irritation, poor concentration, technical impediments of body or writing material, or positive adverse factors inherent in the purpose of the manuscript, the contents, or the effect of names and associations or of the person of the recipient. All these causes have to be accounted for and interpreted in a graphological analysis.

Our main fields of investigation will be as has just been said:

(*a*) Investigation of the guiding image, the visual patterns which the writer wants to imitate when writing (*eidetic graphology*);

(*b*) investigation of the measure of success a writer achieves through his personal rhythm, his movements, the coordination of his impulses, and the harmony between vision, impulse and execution (*kinaesthetic graphology*).

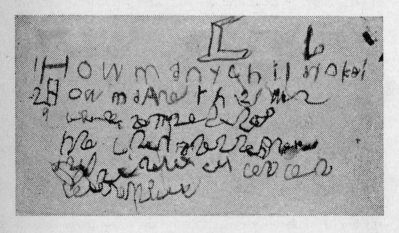

EXAMPLE I

Inability to combine particular directed movements with natural general movements and personal rhythm. Eight-year-old boy of low intelligence.

THE CHILDRENS BRER RABBIT
looked just the doors and there he saw Brer
Fox sitting up in a rocking chair all wrapped
up in frannel and looking very weak. Brer
Rabbit looked all arounds but he could and
any dinner

EXAMPLE 2

Inability to separate the images of different words or to harmonize them with personal rhythm. Eleven-year-old boy of subnormal intelligence.

We are in a big field.
See the pretty little chicks.
See the big pig.
What pretty roses.
We will get roses for Mother
She will love to put the roses
in water

EXAMPLE 3

This eight-year-old boy finds it very hard to combine particular movements with his general personal rhythm.

She will get water in
the pail pail.
We are so happy by.
the sea,

EXAMPLE 4

An eight-year-old boy who finds it hard to master the movement images of the alphabet. Note repetition of the word "pail".

Once upon a time there was a piece of wood. It happened to be in the shop of an old carpenter. whose name was Mr. Cherry.

EXAMPLE 5

An eleven-year-old boy has trouble connecting his letters.

My bicycle has two wheels.
Each wheel has a rubber tyre.
I pump up my tyre
to make them hard.

EXAMPLE 6

Very fair mastery of movement images by a ten-year-old girl. Note hesitations over L of bicycle and pu of pump, and exaggerated distance between words.

CHAPTER II

GUIDING IMAGE
AND EXECUTING MOVEMENT

EXCEPT in a few experiments where the graphologist is able to watch and to observe the writer while he produces a manuscript, the material provided for analysis is an already finished manuscript, the graphic trace on the paper. From this, the graphologist has to reconstruct the two basic elements in the writer who produced it: his guiding images (which are, as we have just found, movement images) and his actual movements when writing.

Before we start to investigate and single out all the various aspects and interpretations of guiding images which form the contents of this book, we have to make a clear, theoretical discrimination between the image and the executing movement. In actual writing this is not so easy, because the final manuscript contains both. Even single features like, for instance, the thickness of the stroke, may be partly, or in some cases, due to the writer's liking of the impression produced by it, and partly due to the peculiarity of his physical powers and impulses.

Just as personality and character are only facets of the body-mind unit, so is the actual writing, the visual matter fixed on the paper, only one facet of another unit in which image and executing movement are two other parts. The executing movement itself we have to divide again into nervous impulse on the one hand, and muscular action on the other. In this combination of four different processes of writing the image represents a creative pattern, the nervous impulse the creative force, the actual muscular action the act of creation, and the actual manuscript the product of it, the finished creation.

Here are some other suggestive descriptions which make clearer the distinction between these four elements:

(1) *The Guiding Image:* Platonic idea, life plan, conception, purpose, vision, perception, *Gestalt* principle, inner status,

orientation in space, organizing centre, configuration pattern, focus, motive, model, Freud's "Id", Aristotle's "entelecheia".

(2) *The Nervous Impulse:* Impetus, life force, efficacy, spirit, impulse, personal rhythm, *élan* (Bergson's *élan vital*), push, dynamics, vitality, degree of participation in life, creative strength, power, individual motor sense, emotion.

(3) *The Muscular Faction:* Means, execution, work, grip, formalization, way, application, realization in time, projection, actual configuration, radiation, gesture, painting.

(4) *The Actual Manuscript:* End, achievement, effect, result, gain, construction, *Gestalt*, trace, syndrome, frozen movement, expression, form, manifestation, appearance, portrait.

To overcome elements of antagonism and resistance from inside and outside each writer has to struggle against them in the writing process. The image of this struggle also appears in the writing.

CHAPTER III

SOURCES OF IMAGES

BEFORE we discuss a list of writing trends and the guiding images and interpretations implied, let us get a clear picture of whence these images come, by what techniques they can be traced, and by what methods we are able to interpret them. From the first chapter we already know that these images have developed from visual images into movement images, into automatized patterns of writing gestures.

The first element of the image is, of course, the standard form. This is, in writing, the copybook form of the alphabet, the standard form of words and the standard shape of the manuscript. Copybook forms and methods of teaching differ in different countries. The modern way of teaching writing in Britain is first to teach the reading and writing of separate letters and, later, to teach cursive writing and the connecting of letters. The most popular copybooks for writing were in earlier days the books by Pitman, and today the books by Mary Richardson (University of London Press Ltd.). In America writing styles differ in many respects. The most popular American textbook is the Palmer Method (Palmer Company) Ltd. French writing style is rounder than ours. In Central Europe sizes and proportions are different, and the writing slants to the right. In Canada they use more or less the American style. South African writing slants to the right. Australian writing has some English, some American characteristics.

The form of a manuscript as a whole is determined by the size and shape of the paper and by its purpose: whether it is a private letter, business letter, application form, postcard, address on an envelope, poem, note, etc. The manuscript form is also conditioned by the standard forms of different countries and classes.

Deviations from copybook forms and other typical patterns arise from the following causes:

(1) Imitation.

(2) Suggestions originating in the writer's imagination:
    (*a*) Colours.
    (*b*) Content of words and sentences and the associations connected with them.
    (*c*) Environment.
    (*d*) The purpose of the actual manuscript.
    (*e*) The addressee of the letter and the writer's approach to him.

The overriding factor, however, is always the writer's personal experience of space, his individual organizing ability, his sense of order and disorder, of rhythm and repetition, of the relations between things and persons, of periodicity and cycles, of sympathy and antipathy, of his own position in the world, and his attitude to today, tomorrow and yesterday. It will depend on his personal experience of conflict and harmony, inclination and disinclination, on what he finds beautiful, easy and useful, or on what he dislikes and wishes to eliminate from his writing. I shall deal with all these elements in the following chapters.

These deviations will work on the formation of every letter or part of a letter, every word, every manuscript as a whole.

To assist the graphologist in his work of interpretation and research, the following methods and principles may be observed.

The first principle of research is the purely empirical one of accumulating, observing and comparing and cataloguing handwritings of people whose qualities are known. Observation and comparison will always be the basis of any science. It is amazing how close the statistical approach of some experimentalists approaches to these basic methods.

Then there is the greatly overrated experimental method which involves letting people write under fixed conditions and checking up on the results.

The most important principle of interpretation of the writing image is, however, of a symbolic nature. Our first guide is the language; when we describe any writing quality we already describe in some way a quality or a complex of qualities belonging to the writer. By the psycho-analytical method of free association connected with the word describing the writing trend we get a lot of results. The guiding images are in the centre of our personality;

they are the guiding principles, the pattern forms of our personality, and all our expressions and projections can be traced back
to this centre. This principle of analogy of expression is a basic
principle of graphology and of any psychology of expression. We
must always realize that writing is a projection and a fixation of
gestures and movements which have a meaning.

Language is our foremost instrument of conscious expression,
and it is full of symbolic references and suggestive associations.
To explain myself more clearly: the analogy is easy to follow when
we say that somebody writes tidily or fussily and so deduce that
he must be tidy or fussy. There is, however, a reservation to be
made, since some of our expressions are influenced by cross-
motives which, for instance, may make a quick man write slowly
in a particular instance.

Some other descriptions of writing trends are limited to a
pictorial symbol or complex of symbols which then has to be
further elaborated. When we say that somebody's lines rise or fall,
that he writes sharply, or that he writes with a forward or backward inclination, there are associative suggestions, *Gestalt* suggestions of hopes or ambitions rising or falling, of a sharp wit or of
a sharpening attitude, an indication that the writer looks forward
to the future, or that he is disinclined to do so and has a tendency
to look back and hold on to the past.

The illustrations *A* to *H* may help you to understand the imagery
behind the gestures of different writers. When we copy somebody's
writing we imitate unconsciously his attitude, and this may help
us to understand his guiding images.

The laws of interpreting pictures, forms, direction and extensions and their symbolic content are developed according to
different psychologies: the psychology of aesthetics (empathy),
symbolism of art, *Gestalt* psychology and, of course, the different
schools of depth psychology with their profound knowledge of
symbols, suggestions and influences.

Characterology has also helped to infer the presence of one
quality from the presence of others.

Klages gave the following general definition of expression:
"Every expression is for him the manifestation of a move of the
Psyche, definable by its force, its length of time and its direction
(centrifugal or centripetal)."

So, from many sources, modern graphology has learnt to assess the guiding images of a man, which are the very centre of his personality, and to interpet them in common language, as will be seen from the following chapters. I start with a list of writing tendencies, the guiding images involved and the basic and derivative interpretations.

A

REGULAR WRITING:
Regularity of behaviour

B

IRREGULAR WRITING:
Unsettled behaviour

C

RHYTHMIC WRITING:
Harmonious oscillation between tension and relaxation

D

FULL WRITING:
Imagination

E

LEAN WRITING:
Sobriety

F

RISING LINE:
Ambition
DROPPING LINE:
Despondency

G

WELL LAID-OUT WRITING:
Coordination

H

UNCOORDINATED WRITING:
Lack of preconceived plans

England

EXAMPLE 7
Large writing

england

EXAMPLE 8
Small writing

London

EXAMPLE 9
Broad writing

London

EXAMPLE 10
Narrow writing

Berlin

EXAMPLE 11
Growing size

Max

EXAMPLE 12
Capital letter growing in size

Berlin

EXAMPLE 13
Diminishing size

Max

EXAMPLE 14
Capital letter diminishing in size

England

EXAMPLE 15
Good proportions

England

EXAMPLE 16
Exaggerated capital letter

England.

EXAMPLE 17
Upper-length emphasized

england

EXAMPLE 18
Upper-length degenerated

England

EXAMPLE 19
Under-length degenerated

England

EXAMPLE 20
Under-length exaggerated

Paris - Berlin

EXAMPLE 21
Rising line

Paris - Berlin

EXAMPLE 22
Straight line

Berlin - Paris

EXAMPLE 23
Drooping line

Berlin - Paris

EXAMPLE 24
Twisting line

Dr Eric Singer

EXAMPLE 25
Convex arc

Dr Eric Singer

EXAMPLE 26
Concave arc

Afghanistan

EXAMPLE 27
Upright angle

Afghanistan

EXAMPLE 28
Slant to the right

Afghanistan

EXAMPLE 29
Slant to the left

Iran

EXAMPLE 30
Right movement (right tendencies)

Iran

EXAMPLE 31
Left movement (left tendencies)

Kindergarten

EXAMPLE 32
Straightforward writing

Kindergarten

EXAMPLE 33
Roundabout writing

Paris

EXAMPLE 34
Changing angle

Interpretation

EXAMPLE 35
Connected writing

Interpre tation

EXAMPLE 36
Disconnected writing

Abercornplace

EXAMPLE 37
Continued writing

A bercorn place

EXAMPLE 38
Discontinued writing

Berlin

EXAMPLE 39
Punctuated writing

Kindergarten

EXAMPLE 40
Rhythmic writing

Kindergarten

EXAMPLE 41
Arrhythmic writing

Paris

EXAMPLE 42
Thick stroke

Paris

EXAMPLE 43
Thin stroke

Paris

EXAMPLE 43a
Artificial changes from thin to thick

Paris

EXAMPLE 44
Plastic stroke

Paris

EXAMPLE 45
Flat stroke

M a

EXAMPLE 46
Framed stroke

M a

EXAMPLE 47
Overflowing (pasty) stroke

Berlin

EXAMPLE 48
Angular connection

Berlin

EXAMPLE 49
Copybook form of connection

Berlin

EXAMPLE 50
Garland connection

Berlin

EXAMPLE 51
Arcade connection

Berlin

EXAMPLE 52
Wavy line connection

Berlin

EXAMPLE 53
Thread connection

Singer

EXAMPLE 54
Simplified writing

Singer

EXAMPLE 55
Complicated writing

Mantua

EXAMPLE 56
Loops

Mantua

EXAMPLE 57
Knots

Ring

EXAMPLE 58
Monotonous writing

Ring

EXAMPLE 59
Varied (original) writing

London

EXAMPLE 60
Elliptic forms

London

EXAMPLE 61
Open o's

London

EXAMPLE 62
Spirals

London

EXAMPLE 63
Square writing

Kindergarten

EXAMPLE 64
Articulated writing

Kindergarten

EXAMPLE 65
Unarticulated writing

Afghanistan

EXAMPLE 66
Crossed writing

Afghanistan

EXAMPLE 67
*Crossed in the wrong
direction or double-crossed*

Afghanistan

EXAMPLE 68
Uncrossed writing

CHAPTER IV

GUIDING IMAGES
AND THEIR INTERPRETATION

GUIDING images are already in existence long before the person starts to learn writing. In fact, the first clumsy scribbles and strokes of an infant already reveal some of its basic conceptions of space.

In the following the guiding images behind some of the basic writing trends are listed and the source meanings as well as the other interpretations deriving from these source meanings are catalogued. The writing trends are all illustrated by examples. Definitions of each trend, however, are only given where such definitions are not included in my other books, *Graphology for Everyman* or *The Graphologist's Alphabet*.

TRENDS OF EXTENSION

LARGE WRITING (Example 7).

Guiding Image: Extension into heights and depths.

Source Meaning: Subjectivism. Intention to develop into the full heights and depths of one's own personality.

Derivative Interpretations: Desire for greatness or real greatness. Development of personality. Individualism. Idealism. Desire to excel others. Leadership. Sense of adventure. Courage. Generosity. Lack of realism, of adjustability and accuracy. Lack of inhibitions, of discipline or consideration and of a sense of proportion. Optimism, pride. Childishness, extravagance, lack of space restrictions. Work on the stage, on the orator's rostrum. Living in high rooms. Work in the open air.

Habitual writing of upper class and stage people and of people living in the open air, as of children (Examples 1, 4).

Pathological Forms: Mania and megalomania, long-sightedness.

SMALL WRITING (Example 8).

Guiding Image: Contraction.

Source Meaning: Contraction of personality.

Derivative Interpretations: Realistic economy of strength. Accuracy. Objectivity and interest in a topic for its own sake. Modesty. Discipline. Realism. Adjustability. Economy. Petti-ness. Lack of personality and magnanimity. Intolerance. Lack of space (living in small rooms, crowded offices, necessity for economy).

Habitual writing of middle class, small office workers.

Pathological Forms: Depression. Inferiority complexes. Parkin-son's disease. Short-sightedness.

BROAD WRITING (Example 9).

Guiding Image: Lateral subjective extension.

Source Meaning: Subjective demand for wider living space.

Derivative Interpretations: Expansiveness. Social extension. Mixing. Desire for travel. Broad views. Broad talking. Claim to broad living space. Lack of consideration and social inhibitions. Broad spending and demanding. Sincerity. Lack of self-control. Weak discipline.

Pathological Forms: Maniac. Hysterical talker.

NARROW WRITING (Example 10).

Guiding Image: Restriction of lateral expansion.

Source Meaning: Dislike of social expansion.

Derivative Interpretations: Discipline. Self-control. Modera-tion. Inhibition. Narrowness of views. Meanness.

Pathological Forms: Inhibitions. Irrational fears. Compulsion neurosis.

GROWING WORDS AND CAPITALS (Examples 11, 12).

Guiding Image: Looking upwards.

Source Meaning: Looking upwards to others.

Derivative Interpretations: Childishness. Naïveté. Inferiority feelings. Frankness. Ambition. Jealousy. Envy. Comparison of self with superiors.

Habitual writing of children and ambitious people of low social background.

Pathological Forms: Backwardness. Inferiority complexes. Pathological jealousy.

DIMINISHING WORDS AND CAPITALS (Examples 13, 14).

Guiding Image: Looking downwards.
Source Meaning: Looking downwards on others.
Derivative Interpretations: Superiority feelings. Pride. Maturity. Diplomacy. Insincerity.

DISPROPORTIONATE EXTENSION OF MIDDLE-, UPPER- AND UNDER-LENGTH (Examples 16–20).

Guiding Image: Lack of sense of proportion and balance.
Source Meaning: Preponderance of the exaggerated, neglect of the underdeveloped parts. Meaning of different parts:
Middle Zone: Normality of self-assertion, of common sense, sentimental, rational and social inclinations.
Upper Length: Extension over everyday life into dreams and speculations.
Underlength: Extension into the subconscious, material and sexual.
Capital Letters: Love of limelight. Over-compensation. Self-dramatization.
Pathological Forms: Lack of balance with different emphasis. Changing size in different parts of the manuscript: cyclic disease. Manic depression.

DIRECTION TRENDS

RISING LINE (Illustration *F* and Example 21).

Guiding Image: Rising.
Source Meaning: Intention to rise.
Derivative Interpretations: Hopefulness. Optimism. Ambition. Aggression. Euphoria. Excitability.
Pathological Forms: Manic stages. Liver troubles.

STRAIGHT LINE (Example 22).

Guiding Image: Straight basis.
Source Meaning: Constancy of basis.
Derivative Interpretations: Straightness. Discipline. Will-power. Constancy of purpose. Inflexibility. Responsibility. Realism.

DROPPING LINE (Illustration *F* and Example 23).

Guiding Image: Going down.
Source Meaning: Feeling of going down.
Derivative Interpretations: Tiredness. Depression. Pessimism. Scepticism. Critical approach. Coming down to earth. Indolence. Apathy.
Pathological Forms: Melancholy. Digestion troubles.

TWISTING LINE: Line going up and down in wavy form (Example 24).

Guiding Image: Waving.
Source Meaning: Wriggling.
Derivative Interpretations: Avoiding of open conflicts. Diplomacy. Trickery. Fraud.

CONCAVE ARC (Example 26).

Guiding Image: Rising after dropping.
Source Meaning: Recovery of strength.
Derivative Interpretations: Successful fight against slackness and depression. Come-back. Recovery of lost ground.

CONVEX ARC (Example 25).

Guiding Image: Rise and fall.
Source Meaning: Fading of initial enthusiasm.
Derivative Interpretations: Quickly disappointed and bored. Gives up too easily. Desire for variety and changes. Multiple interests. Good at making a new start.

UPRIGHT ANGLE (Example 27).

Guiding Image: Standing upright.
Source Meaning: Stability.
Derivative Interpretations: Independence. Living in the present. Reasonableness. Cool judgment. Stable character. Phlegm. Laziness.

RIGHT SLANT (Example 28).

Guiding Image: Leaning forward.
Source Meaning: Leaning towards others and the future.
Derivative Interpretations: Moving forward. Activity. Inclination to get out of own shell. Belief in social achievement. Initiative.

Altruism. Busy character. Escape into activities. Haste. Rest-lessness. Worry. Care for the future. Dependence on others. Weakness.

Pathological Forms: Hysterical over-activity. Gland troubles.

LEFT SLANT (Example 29).

Guiding Image: Leaning back.

Source Meaning: Holding back.

Derivative Interpretations: Disinclination to get out of own shell. Desire for protection and security. Introspection. Fear. Affecta-tion. Playing for safety. Lack of sincerity. Contemplation. Mother-ties.

Pathological Forms: All kinds of complexes based on mother-ties and early experiences.

MOVES TO THE RIGHT (Right Tendencies) (Example 30).

Guiding Image: Stretching out.

Source Meaning: Giving away or fighting off.

Derivative Interpretations: Altruism. Achievement. Construc-tive approach. Enterprise. Efficiency. Aggressiveness. Putting plans into effect. Lack of contemplation.

LEFT MOVES (Left Tendencies) (Example 31).

Guiding Image: Bringing home.

Source Meaning: Collecting.

Derivative Interpretations: Contemplation. Egoism. Greed. Retreat. Introspection. Introversion.

DIRECT WRITING. By direct writing we mean that the writer directs his up-and-down movements in a straight, direct way without unnecessary roundabout movements. In direct writing the actual and the invisible ideal connection between two points agree (Example 32).

Guiding Image: Aiming.

Source Meaning: Aiming at a goal.

Derivative Interpretations: Awareness of purpose. Direction of thought and action towards a goal. Concentration. Will-power. Efficiency. Lack of leisure.

ROUNDABOUT WRITING. By roundabout writing we mean that the writer indulges in roundabout movements or changes the direction of his movements (Example 33).

Guiding Image: Indulging in movements at the cost of direction, or uncertainty of movements and direction owing to lack of guiding image.

Source Meaning: Aimlessness. Uncertainty about aims, or competing aims.

Derivative Interpretations: Indulgence in intellectual fancies. Sense of humour. Lack of direction. Intellectual difficulties. Uncertainty of aim.

Pathological Forms: Change of direction frequent in most forms of mental disease.

CHANGING ANGLE (Example 34).

Guiding Image: Changing inclinations.

Source Meaning: Conflicting inclinations.

Derivative Interpretations: Frequent change in social approach. Liveliness. Lack of steadiness. Many interests. Originating from parents of different temperament without integration of their contrasting characters.

Pathological Forms: Neurotic changes of behaviour. Lack of integration.

CONTINUITY TRENDS

CONNECTED WRITING (Example 35).

Guiding Image: Chain.

Source Meaning: Smooth, logical thought procedure.

Derivative Interpretations: Good faculty of logical deduction and reason. Braininess. Concentration. Adaptability. Good memory. Fanaticism.

Pathological Form: Obsessions.

DISCONNECTED WRITING (Example 36).

Guiding Image: The whole consists of parts.

Source Meaning: Intuitive way of thinking.

Derivative Interpretations: Many ideas. Imagination. Sense of detail. Realism. Jumpy way of thinking. Bad memory. Lack of adjustability. Distraction.

Pathological Forms: Loss of memory. Disintegration of personality.

CONTINUED WRITING. By continued writing I mean that, whether the writing is connected or disconnected, the writer shows no break in his writing impulse. Each stroke aims at the next stroke, each word at the following word. Imagined invisible connections between two words or two letters drawn in the air reveal an inner link (Example 37).

Guiding Image: Link.

Source Meaning: Linking of parts of life and life impulses.

Derivative Interpretations: Sound development. Integration, coordination and continuity of experience, thought and action.

DISCONTINUED WRITING. By discontinued writing I mean writing which shows, whether the writing is connected or not, breaks in the writing impulse. Such breaks may be disproportionate holes between letters, whether outwardly connected, mended or open. There may be changes of direction of the pen, resting-points or mistakes in connection. In discontinued writing the invisible connection will always be bad. Bad, invisible connections between words fall also under this headline (Example 38).

Guiding Image: Lack of guiding image. Breaks in guiding images or uncertainty about guiding images.

Source Meaning: Discontinuity of thought and action.

Derivative Interpretations: Black-outs of memory. Difficulties of logical reasoning, of intelligence, of a psychological nature and of adjustment.

Pathological Forms: Backwardness. Loss of memory. Disintegration of personality.

PUNCTUATED WRITING. By punctuated writing we understand a writing where the pen either inside or outside the stroke rests for a moment, in this way producing unnecessary dots and spots (Example 39).

Guiding Image: Resting.

Source Meaning: Desire or necessity for a pause.

Derivative Interpretations: Resting on laurels. Unwillingness to go on. Black spots in the past. Pause for rest or contemplation. Strong inner tension without outlet. Irritability. Security desire.

Pathological Forms: The unrelaxed tension of psychopathic

people. Also very frequent in writing of violent criminals and murderers.

RHYTHMIC WRITING (Illustration *C* and Example 40).
Guiding Image: Harmony.
Source Meaning: Harmonious alteration between tension and relaxation.
Derivative Interpretations: Grace. Agreement of motor impulses with movements. Taking full part in life. Mental health and balance. Readiness for personal experiences. Smooth solution of conflicts. Full dimension of personality. *Amor fati.*

ARRHYTHMIC WRITING (Example 41).
Guiding Image: Lack of harmony.
Source Meaning: Unsolved conflicts.
Derivative Interpretations: No proportion between tension and outlet. Inability to take full part in life. Weak faculty of experience and feeling. Disharmony in dimensions of personality.
Pathological Forms: Frequent in almost every mental illness and almost habitual in the handwriting of criminals.

COORDINATION TRENDS

COORDINATED WRITING (Illustration *G*).
Guiding Image: Seeing the whole and the parts as well.
Source Meaning: Coordination.
Derivative Interpretations: Clear conception of the relations between whole and parts. Faculty of planning, coordinating, disposing, arranging and organizing. Clear-mindedness. Sense of proportion. Cool head. Analysing brain. Lack of spontaneity. Single items to watch for good or bad coordination:
  Left Margin: Constancy of behaviour, manners and economy.
  Right Margin: Ability to dispose of space and time. Readiness or unreadiness to go on in life. Degree of willingness to leave space uncovered. Economizing or wasting.
  Top Margin: Degree of orthodoxy of behaviour.
  Bottom Margin: Faculty of making decisions in good time and striking out along new lines or, if going too deep down, indulging in sentimentalities and postponing decisions.
  Paragraphing: Organizing of time-table. Correct use of time.

Punctuation: Accuracy or neglect. Pedantry or eccentricity. Underlining: Emphasizing of own point of view.

Spacing between words: Relationship with and estimate of others. If exaggerated: upper-class writing and writing of intellectuals, isolation, ivory tower, losing grip, snobbery, intellectual pride. If crowded: warmth, sympathy, obtrusiveness, lack of tact, living close to others, inability to be alone, low-class writing.

Distance between lines: clarity of mind, judgment in respect of objects. If exaggerated: loss of grip.

Mingling of lines: Being strongly involved in some objects. Carelessness about consequences. Potential muddle. Strong link with the subconscious.

UNCOORDINATED WRITING (Illustration *H*).

Guiding Image: Seeing parts more than the whole.

Source Meaning: Lack of preconceived plans.

Derivative Interpretation: Starting from scratch without planning. Vague disposition of space and time. Genuineness. Experience by trial and error. Lack of sense of proportion.

Special Features: Dislocation of single items, e.g. putting strokes into the middle zone which belong to the upper zone or lower zone. Special taboos and idiosyncrasies, an effort to change nature of things.

COLOURING AND SHADING TRENDS

With the exception of rhythm all the writing trends so far dealt with are based mainly on the visual sense, on the visual experience of space, on the guiding image. Colouring and shading, the character of the stroke itself is of course also influenced by this guiding image, but at the same time pressure plays an important part, this, like rhythm, being mainly the consequence of the motor impulse and of the sense of touch of the writer. When we deal here under the heading of the "guiding image" with the colouring and shading of the stroke, we deal only with that part of it which is the result of the writer's conscious or unconscious desire to produce this particular stroke, that is, which corresponds to his guiding image.

The involuntary achievement of a particular colouring and

shading, the character of the stroke which is conditioned by the writer's personal touch and movement, is outside the scope of this book. It may be added that the character of certain strokes, thin or thick, can be produced in different ways, either by pressure or by the choice of writing instrument or by the writer's way of holding the pen. (Other trends like the rhythm or the plastic character of the stroke can never be deliberately produced if the corresponding impulses are not there.) Although the effect may in some cases be the same, the reason and therefore the explanation is different—which makes rhythm and character of the stroke (pressure) the most complex and difficult aspect of graphology. It may here also be mentioned that while thickness or thinness, framed or overflowing stroke, can be assessed by measurement like all characteristic deviations from the copybook standard and based on the visual sense, it is much more difficult to standardize degrees of pressure, plasticity and rhythm for which no copybook standard exists and which are the results of a difference in movement (motor system) and sense of touch. It is of course possible in writing experiments by using a balance, like the famous Kraepelin weighing machine, invented by the well-known Swiss psychiatrist. Here let us confine ourselves to the guiding images.

THICK WRITING (Example 42).
   Guiding Image: Colourfulness.
   Source Meaning: Inclination to strong sensual effects.
   Derivative Interpretations: Liking for the colourful and sensual, in nature, food, drink and sex. Artistic, imaginative. Forceful, heavy, primitive, brutal.

THIN WRITING (Example 43).
   Guiding Image: Black-white picture.
   Source Meaning: Seeing the basic lines, abstract thinking.
   Derivative Interpretations: Abstraction, lack of sensuality, intellectualism.

PLASTIC (LIVELY) WRITING (Example 44). We define plastic writing as a writing where the stroke shows rhythmic variation of pressure and where the writing makes a plastic and lively impression. An artificial alternation between thin and thick strokes like that in Example 43*a* is not plastic at all.

Guiding Image: Plastic three-dimensional picture.
Source Meaning: Full participation in life.
Derivative Interpretations: Complexity, depth of experience in feelings, readiness for experience, integration, vitality, emotional balance.

FLAT WRITING (Example 45). By flat writing I mean a stroke without any vitality or rhythm, which makes no plastic impression at all.

Guiding Image: Two-dimensional flat picture.
Source Meaning: Lack of full participation in life.
Derivative Interpretations: Lack of feeling and sympathy. Emotional apathy. Cinderella feelings.
Pathological Forms: Melancholy, schizophrenia, criminal tendencies.

FRAMED STROKE (Example 46). By framed stroke I mean a stroke where the two margins are clearly shaped, coherent and consistent.

Guiding Image: Clear shape.
Source Meanings: Consistency. Coherence.
Derivative Interpretations: Firmness, no ambiguity, clarity, substance, concentration, resistance to temptations.

OVERFLOWING (PASTY) STROKE (Example 47).

Guiding Image: Blurred, uncertainty of frontiers between objects.
Source Meaning: Sensuality.
Derivative Interpretations: Love of pleasure, food, drink, sex, colours, nature. Artistic temperament, untidiness, lack of neatness.
Pathological Forms: Addicts, alcoholics, digestion troubles.

FORM

ANGULAR CONNECTION (Example 48).

Guiding Image: Straight and sharpening.
Source Meaning: Straight way to the point of decision.
Derivative Interpretations: Awareness of conflicts, facing conflicts. Topical, objective, reliable, hard-working, resistant, tense, hard, sharp, uncompromising, cruel.
Pathological Form: Sadism.

COPYBOOK FORM (Example 49).

Guiding Image: Imitation of copybook.
Source Meaning: Conventionality.
Derivative Interpretations: Orthodoxy, adaptation to circumstances. Yes-man, lack of imagination and personality, humdrum.
Pathological Form: Pathological or criminal lack of personality and feelings.

GARLAND CONNECTION (Example 50).

Guiding Image: Round and open (garland-shaped).
Source Meaning: Pleasant and sincere.
Derivative Interpretations: Friendliness, kindness, naturalness, lack of formality, easy-going, adjustable, thoughtless, lazy.

ARCADE CONNECTION (Example 51).

Guiding Image: Round and closed (arcade-shaped).
Source Meaning: Diplomacy.
Derivative Interpretations: Formal, polite, standardized, insincere, perfectionist, building up himself according to a personality-ideal (saint, model man), liar, fraud.

WAVY LINE CONNECTION (Example 52).

Guiding Image: Wavy.
Source Meaning: Avoidance of sharpness.
Derivative Interpretations: Diplomacy, adaptability, versatility, quick changes, suggestibility, impressionability, evasion, lying.

THREAD CONNECTION (Example 53).

Guiding Image: Gliding.
Source Meaning: Avoiding decisions.
Derivative Interpretations: Gliding through, highest degree of impressionability and suggestibility, versatility, lack of decisiveness, lack of character and single purpose, dishonesty.
Pathological Forms: Hysteria; every form of disintegration of personality.

REGULAR WRITING (Illustration *A*).

Guiding Image: Symmetry.
Source Meaning: Regularity of behaviour.
Derivative Interpretations: Will power, discipline, consideration,

reliability, lack of imagination and enterprise, dullness, queueing spirit, monotony. Habitual writing of disciplined professions (soldiers, civil servants, etc.).

IRREGULAR WRITING (Illustration *B*).

Guiding Image: Variety.

Source Meaning: Change of behaviour.

Derivative Interpretations: Love of variety, individuality, moodiness, lack of consideration and discipline, lack of will-power, drift.

SIMPLIFIED WRITING (Example 54).

Guiding Image: Simplification.

Source Meaning: Intelligence, objectivity, faculty of seeing essentials, cultivated taste, matter-of-fact approach, scientific spirit. Natural behaviour.

Neglected Forms: Untidiness, lack of consideration, weakness, concealment, lack of sincerity and reliability.

COMPLICATED WRITING (Example 55).

Guiding Image: Ornaments.

Source Meaning: Complication, style.

Derivative Interpretations: Love of complication, traditions, formalism, fussiness, cumbersome approach, lack of objectivity.

Pathological Forms: Obsessions, hallucinations, persecution mania.

FULLNESS OF WRITING (Illustration *D*).

Guiding Image: Embracing.

Source Meaning: Imagination.

Derivative Interpretation: Individualism, subjectivity, dreaminess, artistic spirit, fullness of life, universal approach.

LEANNESS OF WRITING (Illustration *E*).

Guiding Image: Seeing individual forms without space between.

Source Meaning: Sobriety.

Derivative Interpretations: Singling out some features of the whole, objectivity, realism, dullness, dryness, academic views, specialist spirit.

MONOTONOUS WRITING (Example 58). By monotonous writing I mean that the writer has only one form for each letter.

Guiding Image: Limited number of guiding images.

Source Meaning: Lack of imagination.

Derivative Interpretations: Monotony, dullness, drabness, lack of intelligence, pedant, bore.

Pathological Forms: Present in the writings of many psychopaths.

VARIETY IN WRITING (Example 59). By variety in writing I mean that the writer has a variety of forms for each letter or most letters.

Guiding Image: Plenty of images.

Source Meaning: Imagination.

Derivative Interpretations: Intelligence, culture, wide interests, intellectual charm, self-taught, adventurer, swindler. (The latter interpretation is confined to the mixing of two different alphabets and copybook forms when there is no natural explanation for it, like the adaptation to a language or a new style in the transition period.)

ELLIPTIC FORMS (Example 60). By elliptic forms I mean circular letters drawn in an elliptic form.

Guiding Image: Elliptic.

Source Meaning: Interests and motives centred round more than one focus.

Derivative Interpretations: Many-sided interests, lack of sure instinct, lack of clear instinctive choice, hesitation, lack of decision.

OPEN CIRCLES (Example 61). By open circles I understand a form where the circular letters (o, a, d, etc.) are not closed.

Guiding Image: Openness.

Source Meaning: Indiscretion

Derivative Interpretations: Sincerity, talkativeness, unreliability.

SPIRALS (Example 62). By spirals I understand spiral-like scrolls, either in circular letters or as additional ornaments to other letters.

Guiding Image: Labyrinth.

Source Meaning: Being involved.

Derivative Interpretations: Sense of family, cunning shrewdness, touchiness, vanity, fear of persecution, secretiveness.

Pathological Forms: Fixed ideas, persecution mania, paranoia.

SQUARE FORMS (Example 63). By square forms I understand writing where the round parts are transformed into rectangulars.

Guiding Image: Rectangular.

Source Meaning: Inclination to build.

Derivative Interpretations: Gift for building, mechanical and technical work, preoccupation with houses, liking for firm foundations.

ARTICULATED WRITING (Example 64). By articulated writing I mean the writing of words and sentences so that letters inside words are clearly and distinctly spaced, and so are words.

Guiding Image: Discrimination.

Source Meaning: Articulation of thought and speech.

Derivative Interpretations: Clear thinking, good powers of self-expression, intellectual discrimination.

UNARTICULATED WRITING (Example 65). By unarticulated writing I mean a writing where neither the letters inside words nor the words themselves are clearly spaced.

Guiding Image: Not clear.

Source Meaning: Bad articulation of thought and speech.

Derivative Interpretations: Lack of discrimation, of clear thinking, poor power of self-expression.

CROSSED WRITING (Examples 66, 67). By crossed writing I understand a handwriting where up-strokes or bars cross the down stroke. We have to differentiate between crossings which are normal and prescribed by the copybook and those which are not.

Guiding Image: Crossing a barrier.

Source Meaning: Resolution to cross barriers.

Derivative Interpretations. For normal prescribed crossings: courage, resolution, vigour, self-sacrifice. Lack of consideration (cruelty, if circumstances demand it), activity, aggressive spirit, realism, normality, "courageous sinner". For abnormal crossings not prescribed, including crossings in the wrong direction and double crossings: lack of inhibition to do the extraordinary, unorthodox and abnormal, impudence, rebellious instincts, revolutionary attitude, belief to be a person chosen by fate, driving matters to extremes, force of destruction and self-destruction, perversion.

Pathological Forms: Sexual perversion (under-length) and suicide tendencies (signature).

UNCROSSED WRITING (Example 68). By uncrossed writing I understand a writing style where crossing of lines prescribed by the copybook is avoided by the writer.

Guiding Image: Stopping at a barrier.

Source Meaning: Disheartening effect of barriers.

Derivative Interpretations: Cowardice, caution, reluctance, inhibitions, repression, attempt to shirk duty—sometimes successfully, restraint, meditation, delaying tactics.

Pathological Forms: All kinds of repressions.

CHAPTER V

PICTORIAL WRITING, DOODLING, SCRIBBLING

IN general, handwriting reproduces only the broadest of pictorial characteristics, such as symmetry, vertical or horizontal extension, elliptic or spiral forms, etc.; but some few handwritings show a more definite pictorial character, distinct shapes and suggestions of certain objects. Some of these objects are discernible without any knowledge of the writer's character, mind, occupation or preoccupation; some others only with knowledge of these factors. Here handwriting has something in common with doodling. Both forms of expression are therefore dealt with together in this chapter. Let us take the little pictures in handwriting first.

There are two abnormal forms of pictorial writing. The first is the interruption of the writing by little pictures representing words, as found in the writing of children, of primitives, or of mentally sick persons; or the sticking on to the paper of newspaper or magazine cuttings as a substitute for words, as also found in the writing of paranoiacs and other mentally sick people. The use of more than two different inks in the manuscript gives it also a pictorial character and is also a sign of mental disease. In these cases, however, the meaning of the pictures, which are intentionally, consciously and deliberately used, is still intelligible.

The other abnormal form is a one-man's alphabet. Here the mentally sick person designs his own alphabet, intelligible to no other person. As mental sickness means that a person's thoughts and actions diverge from what is intelligible to persons of the same level of culture and education, this kind of writing is a reliable indication of mental disease.

But pictorial writing does not occur only in the abnormal cases of mentally sick writers. If an image is very strong in an ordinary person's mind it sometimes unconsciously enters his writing. From the point of view of interpretation, these uncommon pictures and their symbolic character should not be over-estimated; but to demonstrate that a person's handwriting is an expression of his mind, they have value. And in some cases they provide special indications.

The most frequent pictures are those that transform letters into figures, musical notes or sexual symbols. Examples 69 to 78 give a fair indication of how clearly and in how many different forms these figures, notes and sexual symbols figure in handwriting.

From the point of interpretation, however, their meaning is very general and ambiguous. Figure writing indicates basically some relationship with figures. It may be that the writer is interested in figures, or familiar with figures or good at figures. It may also be that, although he is neither good, familiar with or interested in them, he has, in connection with his profession, to see figures frequently. It may also imply that, as figures often stand in men's minds for money, he is interested in money.

Statisticians and accountants, mathematicians and business men, but also poor men who dream about money, may be among figure-writers. Saudek points out that figures written in more than two strokes are a sign of a dangerous and often criminal greed for money.

Some graphologists try to interpret figure-writing in the light of numerological symbolism. I do not agree with that, and object in the same way to seeking astrological symbols in handwriting.

Another frequent picture in handwriting is that of musical notes and musical keys. Here, again, it is no sure indication of special talent, only an indication of an interest or some connection with music. The great composer or conductor, as well as the amateur or music-lover, even the printer of music-paper, may show these signs.

Finally, the sexual symbols. Many handwritings show such symbols occasionally, sex and its organs being part of many people's imaginative life. They also will tend to appear in the handwriting of people who by their profession are used to seeing people in the nude, so that their attention is drawn to the shape of the human body (masseurs, secretaries of nudist clubs).

If, however, the writing of these symbols becomes frequent, constant and dominant in a handwriting, it indicates a special attachment to the organs of sex, a lowered resistance to the various

Sex symbols in handwriting

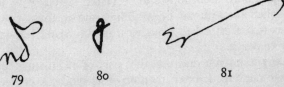

Figure-writing   *Musical notes*

Knives, daggers, whips

forms of sexual cults, excesses or exhibitions. Pictures of organs of the writer's own sex support other indications of homosexuality or lesbianism.

The next most frequent pictures in writing are outlines of instruments, including weapons of assault, such as knives, ropes, daggers, pistols, whips, or the gallows. These appear in the writing of violent or cruel people, of people who contemplate murder or suicide; gallows appear especially in the writings of convicted criminals who expect the gallows, and whips in the writings of masochists and sadists, who dream of such things (Examples 79 to 81). Nevertheless it is impossible to tell how far such dreams lead to actual cruelty, and it is difficult to assess whether such instruments of torture and destruction are directed towards others or towards the writer himself.

All these symbols occur much less in the text of the writing than in or after the signature.

The same applies to instruments or other objects connected with professions or hobbies: scissors in the writing of tailors and cutters, combs in the writing of hairdressers, dentures in the writing of dentists, horses in the writing of riders, bows in the writing of persons whose hobby is archery, aeroplanes in the signatures of pilots, etc. Here again the question remains open whether the symbol betrays the writer's actual profession or hobby or the one the writer is suited to or dreaming about. A picture of teeth may occur in the writing of the dentist as well as of his patient, a picture of ears in the writing of a deaf man as well as of a man whose ugly ears are his tragedy, or of an aurist.

Other types of pictures can be occasionally found relating either to an object of desire or to something else which is strongly in the writer's mind, such as the hammer and sickle in the writings of partisans of Communism. In *A Handwriting Quiz Book* (Example 30) I reproduced somebody's abbreviated signature, a letter *H*, which looked like a human body gliding into an abyss; two months after this manuscript had been written the writer leaped from a window to death.

In many cases you may feel that part of a signature represents a little sketch; but the interpretation of its symbolic content would be pure guesswork without a knowledge of the facts, or an opportunity of questioning the writer. This is a different matter from normal graphological assessment, where the copybook form gives a clear standard for comparison.

Too much arbitrary guesswork is involved in the unmasking of these not completely obvious sketches. As a starting-point for questioning the writer or for the free association technique they may be, however, quite useful. Anyway, they are extremely rare.

The purely intuitive and telepathic graphologists, especially Raphael Schermann, were the first to draw attention to these pictures in writing and showed an amazing talent for discovering and explaining them. Although scientific graphology kept a strong check on this approach, historically it proved quite useful, because it drew the attention of some leading research workers such as Pulver and Anna Mendelssohn to the eidetic, symbolical, pictorial character of writing in general, a tendency which was also strongly

emphasized by the contemporary depth psychology and the discovery of symbols in the subconscious and in dreams.

From these little pictures in handwriting it is but a short distance to that funny habit called "doodling".

It has become a common feature in the Press to reproduce
doodles of well-known people and then to try to interpret the
symbolic content of these little pictures, sometimes with very
sweeping statements leading to more or less prefabricated deductions. Just as in pictorial writing, interpretation of doodles
requires in many cases some knowledge of the personality of the
writer, which may make the deductions biased. These deductions
are in any case less important, less strict and less controlled than
graphological assessment from handwriting. But even so, the laws
of graphology, like other general laws (some drawn from the
Rohrschach test, some from general considerations), can be usefully
applied.

First of all, the graphological rules about pressure, stroke, speed,
angle, direction, size, width, roundness or angularity, regularity
and rhythm, etc., should be taken into account. Fullness or leanness, simplification or ornamentation, spiral, elliptic or square
writing, also retain their basic meanings. Musical notes, figures,
weapons, sexual symbols, etc., can be interpreted in the same way
as in graphology. In addition the following keys to interpretation
can be applied: two-dimensional doodles will show a less plastic
and all-round perception than three-dimensional doodles. Monotonous, repetitive doodles show a lesser degree of imagination than
varied ones. It may also draw attention to some subconscious
fixations.

Static drawings may point to a more static, while dynamic ones
point to a more dynamic personality, either of creative energy or
of restless dissipation. Strokes or arcs only, as different from
pictures of definite objects will disclose a kind of mind which is
less certain of its objects or preferences than one which settles
down to drawing objects. A man who draws faces or human
figures will be more interested in human subjects than one who
draws non-human objects of a technical nature, or flowers, animals
or ornaments.

Here again one must differentiate between doodles which represent something from reality and life and such as come from

imagination and dreams only. It also seems important to note whether a person draws doodles of the whole or a part of his subject, the first pointing to a more general, the latter to a more specialized approach.

The drawing of rectangles should be watched to see whether the bases are broader than the extension to the top, indicating that the writer likes a broad, material basis; or with smaller bases and taller extensions, indicating that the writer "builds castles in the air".

If there are many doodles on the sheet it is significant whether they are centred in the middle of the sheet or spread over the whole; the first indicating concentration, the latter, dissipation of energies. Even a single individual doodling should be examined in the light of whether it is concentrated or dissipated in style.

This leads to the question of framing. If the doodle contains clear ornaments which, of their nature, require a frame; if the whole drawing is a composition of which the frame forms an organic and natural part, framing indicates an orderly, clear, systematic mind, with the faculty of seeing and distinguishing the pattern of things.

If, however, doodles which do not really belong to one another or are so vaguely composed that their coherence is not evident are thrown together in an artificially imposed frame, it shows fear and a desire for protection and security.

Finally, observe whether the doodler leaves his sketch alone when he has finished it and starts something new, or whether he feels an urge to go on adding to it and altering it. This is one of the few factors in doodling which can be judged on their own merits. For it can be certainly said that the doodler who cannot leave well alone is likely to be more closely involved with his work than one who feels free to start something new repeatedly; while the latter will be more relaxed in himself, will be temperamentally inclined to "piece work", a man for whom work is finished when his job is finished. The first type is a more daemonic character, who goes out either for perfection or destruction.

Doodles may also be used as a projection test, giving the analyst an opportunity of letting the free associations of the doodler work and explain his intention; see Illustrations *I* to *V* on pages 51 to 54.

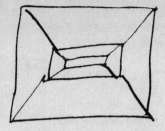

I
*Feeling of fatalism, of being caught
and frustrated by sex and life*

J
Interest in the human race, but not too much kindness

K
*Likes his daily routine work,
one thing after another*

L
Dynamic, colourful, forceful,
creative, restless

M
Good at taking the easy
way out

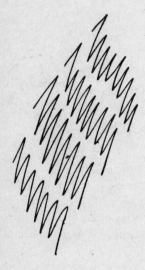

N
Aggressiveness, defensiveness

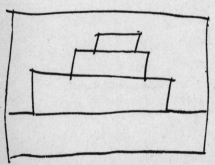

O
Safety first!

P
*Involved design, shrewd, diplomatic,
afraid of persecution*

R
*Ability to see all round an object,
some tension*

S
*Longing for freedom, colour,
nature, expression, relaxation*

T
Rebellious instincts, pugnacity

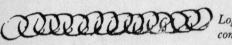

U
Logical, inductive,
consequential

V
Systematic, analytical,
organizing faculty

The graphologist can seldom afford the luxury of interviewing his subject. It is one of the most significant differences of graphology compared with other personality tests and projection methods, that the graphologist does not need the presence of the tested person, and can work without questioning and interviewing.

Doodles are only of minor importance to the graphologist compared with the adult's handwriting, and I would not have elaborated this system of judging doodles if these principles did not also apply to something much more important, that is, the scribbling of infants, to which all the principles just developed can be very usefully applied. In passing, I may mention that a statistical, thorough investigation by one of Saudek's pupils of the handwriting and drawings of school-children has demonstrated that the drawing skill of the child has almost no influence on the character of his handwriting.

CHAPTER VI

EGO-SYMBOLS

WHILE in general the English handwriting style is no easier to analyse than any of the continental ones, it contains one unique opportunity—the word "I". In all other languages the word denominating the Ego, such as the Latin *ego*, the French *moi*, the German *ich*, the Slavonic *ja*, consists of two or more letters, and is written with a small initial. Only in the English language does it consist of one letter only, and this written with a capital. In addition, this letter "I" is very simple in design, sometimes only a straight stroke, clearly denoting that at a time when alphabets were still not divided it also symbolized the figure 1. It is more than probable that the original design suggested the sketch of a single person.

This capital letter "I" symbolizing the ego is bound to evoke in the writer emotions connected with his ego, and is therefore unconsciously conceived as an ego-symbol, as an image of the writer's ego.

Crépieu-Jamin, the great French graphologist, in his experimental book about the bases of graphology, long ago drew attention to the particular role which the writing of the word "I" plays in the interpretation of British and American handwriting. He proved his theory by an experiment. He asked a hundred English people to write the sentence "I was in Iceland", and with the exception of a very small percentage the writing of the word "I" was much more evocative and elaborate than the "I" of "Iceland", or at least different. He went on to speak to the writers about Iceland until they got generally interested in it, and then asked them to write the sentence again. This time they forgot a bit about their egos and the capital letter of "Iceland" became more emphasized than before.

Saudek, the first ambassador of continental graphology in this country, naturally studied the word "I" and made a remarkable

William and I go

EXAMPLE 82
Normal size of word I

William and I go

83 *I exaggerated*

William and I go

84 *I degenerated*

I think I will

85 *Fluctuating use of I*

William and I go

William and I go

86 and 87 *Elaboration of I*

William and I go

88 *Simplification of I*

1 2 7 9

89 *I in figure form*

William and I

90 and 91 *Hesitation and alterations*

William and I

I will

92 *I slanting back, the "guilty"*

contribution to its interpretation. He, however, confined himself to its size. A complex study of this subject should take into account not only size and breadth, but also form, speed, amendments, angle and distance from other words.

Size and breadth: if a comparison of the size of the word "I" with a normal capital letter shows that both are written in the same way, it proves that there is no special emphasis, no inferiority feeling, about the ego. Exaggeration in the size of the word "I" shows a self-conscious over-emphasis and self-dramatization; a diminution in size of the word "I" reveals inferiority. Fluctuations in the size of the word show fluctuations of self-esteem, self-consciousness and self-assertion (Examples 82 to 85).

Form: if the "I" shows different and more elaborate forms than the normal capital letter, it also points to strong self-consciousness, while an "I" in the form of a simple stroke shows at the same time a straightforward approach and personal culture (Examples 86 to 88).

For the interpretation of the different forms of elaboration the general rules of graphological interpretation should be used. The word "I" in figure form, for instance, shows connection of the ego with figures or money. As already mentioned, I disagree with any numerological interpretation (Example 89).

Speed: Freud's rules about writing mistakes are applicable to any hesitation (trembling, breaks, changes of direction) and amendments in the writing of the word "I", showing an emotional uncertainty in the ego (Examples 90, 91).

Angle: if the word "I" shows a difference of angle in comparison not only with the letter "I" but also with the rest of the writing, it is indicative of a discrepancy between the usual, everyday, social behaviour of the writer and his real ego The general rules apply here as well. Special attention should be given if the word "I" slants backwards whilst the rest of the writing shows an upward trend, or even a slant to the right. Such a word "I" looks like a bowing body (Example 92), and indicates, as I have confirmed in many cases, strong guilt feelings. These are sometimes guilt feelings expressing themselves in a religious way, sometimes in a general psychological attitude, sometimes in a sexual abnormality.

Distance: the distance between the word "I" and other words

may differ from the normal spacing between words in the following
ways:

(*a*) "I" more removed;
(*b*) "I" nearer to previous or following word, even connected
with it;
(*c*) distance fluctuating.

Too little attention has been paid up to now to this particular
aspect. A thorough, systematic investigation, especially a comparison of the writing of mentally unbalanced with normal persons,
may yield amazing results.

(*a*) above points to isolation; (*b*) points to an inability to be alone,
implying all the fears and unsound emotions of a person who is
afraid of solitude; (*c*) points to fluctuations in social behaviour.

While the writing of the "I" is particular to English handwriting, the other ego-symbol, the signature, is common to every
writing-style and language. It is understandable, though for the
graphologist a surprising phenomenon, that laymen always try
their hand on signatures, which are, if you are not content with
a superficial assessment, the most difficult, complex and involved
objects of study; on the other hand, of course, they are one of the
most interesting parts of every manuscript.

The reason that they are interesting as well as difficult is that the
signature is the meeting-point of so many features and tendencies
in handwriting, technical, emotional, social, evocative, representative, juridical, etc., that it requires a very careful analysis to
separate them and to judge each feature on its own merits.

What are the points that are involved in a person's signature?

Let us start with the most obvious fact, that the signature has
something to do with the ego, that there is almost always a text
when there is a signature, and that the writer is freer to manœuvre
as regards extension, proportion, etc., when writing his signature
than when writing the text.

There are many different possibilities:

(*a*) The text is similar to the signature.
(*b*) The signature is bigger, broader, more emphasized and
elaborated than the text.
(*c*) The signature is smaller and more unobtrusive than the text.

In relation to the position of the text:

(*d*) The signature is at a normal distance from the text.
(*e*) It is too close to the text (Example 92*a*).
(*f*) It is too far from the text (Example 92*b*).

In direction:

(*g*) The signature rises (differently from the text) (Example 92*c*).
(*h*) The signature droops (differently from the text) (Example 92*d*).

As regards placing on the sheet and inclination:

(*i*) The signature is pushed to the right (Example 92*e*).
(*j*) The signature is pushed to the left (Example 92*f*).
(*k*) The signature is upright, or slanting backwards, while the text slants to the right (Example 92*g*).
(*l*) The signature slants to the right, while the text is upright or slanting to the left (Example 92*h*).

The fact that the signature is different from the text is in itself indicative of a discrepancy in the writer between his everyday ego and the imagined ego of his dreams. In this respect the signature always represents the imagined ego, if the person has only one type of signature. If there are, however, two types of signature, as is frequent with people in public positions, such as Royalty and other heads of State, it is not difficult to judge which one represents their official ego ("l'homme dehors" as the French graphologists call it) used for signing official and representative documents, and the other one, representing the private ego, used in letters to the writer's family or friends. In *A Handwriting Quiz Book* I have shown the development of Hitler's and Mussolini's handwriting; the difference between their signatures from the time when they were comparatively unknown to the time when they became official persons and men in power.

The second fact that can be deduced from a discrepancy between the writing of the text and of the signature is that there has been some development. In these cases the signature—apart from exceptional cases such as the rise to power of the dictators—reprsents the earlier, the older style, while the text represents the writer's present style. The reason, as already stated, is that too

yours sincerely,
John

　　　　　　　92a Signature too close to the text

yours sincerely,

　　　John

　　　　　　　92b Signature too far removed
　　　　　　　　from the text

yours sincerely,
　　　John

　　　　　　　92c Rising signature

yours sincerely

　　John

　　　　　　　92d Drooping signature

yours sincerely,

　　　John

　　　　　　　92e Signature pushed to the right

yours sincerely,
John

　　　　　　　92f Signature pushed to the left

yours sincerely,

　John

　　　　　　　92g Signature upright, while
　　　　　　　　text slants forward

yours sincerely,

　John

　　　　　　　92h Signature slants forward, while
　　　　　　　　text is upright

frequent changes in a signature would deprive it of its official flavour, of its "rubber stamp" character, as deposited with the bank and known to everybody who has to deal with the writer.

A further reason for less frequent changes in the signature is that the writer is strongly attached emotionally to this ego symbol, with all its early memories, with all the dreams of impressing the world with his name, dreams dating from the time when his signature was first evolved. This fact that the signature is mostly older in origin than the text, for the two reasons mentioned, is, apart from the cases where manuscripts from different stages of development of the writer are available, the only chance the graphologist has of checking the development of the writer, and the history of his character development.

Thus a man whose signature is bigger than his text may have started life with high hopes which have not been realized; while the man whose ordinary handwriting has become bigger than his signature has developed a higher degree of self-confidence than he used to have in earlier days.

In fact, that there is a discrepancy at all between signature and text, between the official ego and the everyday man, is always indicative of a certain insincerity, of a desire to appear outwardly different from the private self. On the other hand, a signature completely similar to the rest of the text is—apart from the easily recognizable cases, where the general standard of the writer is too low to allow him to write down his name in a different way—a very good indication of sincerity and reliability, of conformity and harmony between the official and the private person.

If the signature is bigger and more elaborate than the text it is a hint that where the ego is concerned the degree of self-assertion is much higher than it appears in ordinary life. On the other hand, where the signature is smaller the ego-consciousness is much less developed than is noticeable in ordinary life.

The distance of the signature from the text is relevant and indicative of the attachment of the ego to his surroundings, environment and circumstances. A signature written very close to the text reveals a strong attachment; some way away, it is indicative of unconscious or conscious inner detachment.

The placing on the sheet and the direction are also highly revealing. A rising signature (except with the Dutch, who are taught this way) shows professional ambition; a drooping one, tiredness and depression. Ordinarily, the signature is placed on the right side of the sheet at a fair distance from the right-hand margin. A signature pushed to the extreme right is indicative of an over-active person, of a desire to escape into frenzied activity. On the other hand, a signature written in the middle of the page is a sign of a cautious, diffident attitude, of a desire for security. If it is pushed to the extreme left it is a sign of an exaggerated desire for security and retirement, of a disappointed and escapist attitude, and in extreme cases a sign of suicidal tendencies. A signature written from the extreme left to the extreme right over the whole sheet is a sign of an exaggerated desire for space, indicative of an expansive nature.

We come now to the different parts of the signature, Christian name, surname, titles. Every country has its own customs governing the writing of these different parts of the signature; so has each class, and so have many professions. Schoolboys will write their full names; children their Christian name only; grown-ups in Great Britain, mostly the initials of their Christian names and the full surname. Medical doctors in many countries place their title before their name; other graduates and army officers after the name.

Each part of the name refers to a separate part of the writer's origin, development and character. The Christian name is the most individual one; according to religion, it comes from God and cannot be changed. Where there are several Christian names, one of them is the one by which the person is generally called by his or her friends and family. The surname gives the family origin, the genealogy. Titles are either inherited or acquired. Some titles are professional, and as such belong to the official signature. So the whole history of a person is portrayed in his signature, and any extra emphasis attached to certain parts of it indicates an emphasis which the writer attaches to this special part of his character. People whose emphasis is evenly balanced will write their names in the way generally used in their country. Juvenile persons and those who wish to emphasize the private, family element, and attach importance to their early memories, will emphasize their Christian names in comparison with the surname —sometimes so much so that the surname becomes neglected, illegible, even omitted altogether. Unhappily married wives who changed their surnames when they married; foreigners and other people who do not want to draw attention to their surname will neglect it, write it in an unintelligible way, or even drop it. People who want to be popular or familiar either to the addressee or to everybody; persons in the limelight, like popular actors, politicians, film stars, will always write their Christian names fully and clearly —Winston Churchill, Charlie Chaplin. Some will often write their Christian names only. Humbly born, snobbish people aiming to raise themselves socially, may even overdo it and fire off all their guns in one salvo, as in John Guy Pontefract Jeremy Smith.

The reserved or the matter-of-fact type, who dislikes people becoming too easily familiar with him, will, of course, tend to do the opposite, and sign his name in a formal manner with initials and surname. The surname will be emphasized by those who attach importance to it. Members of noble or famous families, people who have won fame for their surname, will emphasize it.

Titles will be, of course, either emphasized or neglected to the extent to which the writer wants to draw attention to them. At a stage where the writer has reached or meant to have reached general recognition, where his name has become a slogan or is in a category of its own, a writer may even drop his Christian name and titles and, in a mixture of extreme self-assertion and extreme modesty, sign his famous surname only. The great Freud began his career by signing himself "Professor Sigmund Freud". Later he signed himself simply "Freud"; his name has become world-famous, and Christian names did not matter any more.

In some cases, personal circumstances and a special personal attitude to a Christian name have a definite bearing on the writing of the signature. I once found that a man emphasized his Christian name considerably in relation to his surname; when I pointed it out to him he told me that as a child, very much to his dislike, he was always called "Jackie", and it was only when he was grown up that he managed to get himself called by his real Christian name, which in this way had become a symbol of independence for him.

The text of a manuscript fails in its purpose of communicating or preserving information when it is illegible. This does not apply to the signature, because, as already pointed out, the signature has now become mainly a "rubber stamp"; one can always write one's name under it, if it is not already on the letter-heading or known to the addressee.

A legible signature will always be a sign of the writer's sincerity and of his readiness to honour his commitments. An illegible signature, on the other hand, will point to a desire to hide, to evade commitments, to keep mental reservations, even to go back on one's word. In such cases there is also always a desire to make it difficult to imitate one's handwriting. This springs from a desire for protection against forgery. This desire makes an elaborate affair of the signature, and in many cases tends to make it illegible.

Here, also, is the answer to the question so often put to me, why doctors' signatures are mostly illegible. The doctor often has to keep his diagnosis secret from the patient. Just as he used to speak Latin to his colleagues, and still habitually writes his prescription in Latin, he writes rather illegibly in an unconscious desire for concealment.

The signature is more often written by most people than any other word they write, and this results in its often being written in a quicker, more routine or careless manner. This has a double significance for the graphologist. First, if a man who has to sign his signature many times a day still writes it accurately, with every letter clearly elaborated, it points to an almost pedantic attitude and, if the text is similarly clearly written, to reliability. If the text is less clear, his pedantry is more likely to be in respect of things which concern himself only.

Another significant factor is the help which we derive from the signature in interpreting the intelligence of the uneducated classes. Even if the writing, for instance, is still cumbersome from lack of writing experience, the signature may be written with a more experienced hand and may help us to avoid the mistakes which are often made by beginners when assessing the intelligence of people who have little writing experience.

One of the most interesting features of a signature is the opportunity to underline it, to add flourishes, and to elaborate it in hundreds of different ways. Just as with pictorial writing, not every meaning involved can be guessed without knowing the writer. Some of the most frequent symbols added to signatures are listed in the chapter on pictorial writing. We can, therefore, confine ourselves here to the following types of elaboration and emphasis.

Let us take these one by one:

(1) *No addition*. Except in very primitive writing this is the sign of a natural, discriminating person who dislikes any fuss.

(2) *Underlining* is always an emphasis on the individual personality of the writer. It is also a barrier against other people, or at least some groups of other people.

(3) *Roofing strokes* have a protecting character. If the roofing stroke consists in an extension of the first letter over the whole name it has to be interpreted in an active sense indicating a person who is ready to take others under his or her care (and to dominate them), while other roofing strokes point rather to a writer who wants to protect himself and his family from interference by others.

(4) *Ornamental additions* are limitless in number and variety. They come basically from an enjoyment of movement and have to be interpreted according to the general rules explained with ornamental writing, pictorial writing and doodling. They also help sometimes to balance the symmetry of the signature.

(5) *Encircling spirals* come from an exaggerated desire for security. This is the spider's web, set to catch every intruder. Swiss peasants, who live alone in the mountains, have almost universally developed this style of signature. Where such an obvious reason does not exist, spirals round a signature indicate cunning and shrewdness involving others, but also that the writer himself is a prey to fixed ideas, mainly ideas of persecution.

(6) *The addition of a full stop or hyphen*, or stop and hyphen, after the signature is indicative of a person who wants to put a full stop to the contents of the letter, who is conventional and distrustful of anything unorthodox.

(7) *The crossing out of the signature* is a sign of rebellious self-destruction, indicating the possibility of suicide. Placing of the signature away to the left is a further indication of the desire to be rid of life.

(8) *The starting-stroke of the signature extended to the left* is a sign that the writer cannot get rid of his early personal memories of some inner fixations.

(9) *An end-stroke extended to the right* shows a definitely aggressive (if sharpened and rising), generous (if rounded and soft) or

defensive (if straight) attitude. (See also the chapter "The Last Letter" in *The Graphologist's Alphabet*.)

In general it can be said that all writing trends should be interpreted in relation to the writer's ego if they are more marked in the signature than in the text. For example, a strong difference in proportion between capital and small letters in the signature will indicate a strong discrepancy between the desire for self-dramatization and the real degree of self-assertion. In the same way large breaks in a signature indicate breaks in the continuity of development of the writer's character, mostly of a disappointing and negative nature.

The last feature to be considered in connection with signatures is the imitative element in their origin. More than in any other part of his writing, the writer has made it his business to consolidate forms which he considers represent his ego best and most fittingly. As this is mostly done at an early stage of development, a comparison with the signatures of his parents, teachers, siblings, relatives, schoolfellows and even his "pin-ups" will lead to the discovery of the writer's heroes. While a signature quite different from his family's writing will always point to the fact that the writer wants to develop his personality in a different, even antagonistic way, from those of his parents and relations, a very similar writing displays the element of admiration which is involved in imitation, though not necessarily of affection. Sometimes you worship the object of your imitation, but sometimes you try to learn from it just in order to replace it; as some savages wear the heads of the rivals they have slain in order to inherit their magic forces.

Among the imitative factors the standard fashions of forming the signature according to country, class and profession also play their part.

CHAPTER VII

THE PORTRAYAL OF CONFLICTING IMAGES IN HANDWRITING

IT has already been pointed out that a writer's personal experiences of resistance and conflict influence his guiding images.

The special symbols of direction forward or backward, the forms of connection representing the preferred forms of the writer, how he wants to be connected with other people—all these elements combine to reveal how the writer makes up his mind about alternatives in himself and his various conflicts with other people.

If we follow up these important personal indications we finally face four basic types of image and approach, which, however, have to be subdivided. As with every other typology, it must be understood that the infinite variety of human personality can never be forced or compressed into a limited number of types and groups, and that each individual may combine elements of two or more types. Incidentally, these types serve only as a coordinating system for the better orientation for the student.

The four types are:

(1) The conflict type.
(2) The receptive type.
(3) The security type.
(4) The confused type.

(1) By *conflict type* I understand a person who makes a dramatic approach to conflict for its own sake, accepts conflict as necessary and sometimes unavoidable. He is what Luther calls "the brave sinner", the Jacob-type who wrestles with good and evil until a decision is reached. This type has to be subdivided into the active, the fighting, the provocative conflict-type who projects his inner drama outwards, and goes all out for conquest, success and achievement; and the passive conflict type, or resistance type, whose battlefield is his own heart, but who firmly resists any interference with

his own choice. The hard worker will mostly be found among the conflict types. It shows a principally masculine type of approach.

Graphological indications of the conflict type are: angular writing, emphasis on strokes, hooks, connected writing, regular writing, simplified writing, crossing strokes, firmness of stroke, straight or rising lines, triangular forms, knotting, upright or right-hand slant, moves to the right (right tendencies), broken or straight extension of end-strokes, horizontal tension. For the fighting, provocative type, look specially for rising strokes, rising lines, sharpening and broadening strokes, triangular forms and right slant.

(2) By the *receptive type* I understand a person who faces antagonism and conflict by embracing and absorbing it. This is the open, receptive, elastic, principally feminine reaction to life.

Graphological indications of the receptive type are: garland connections, colourful, elastic strokes, fullness. Round, extended end-strokes, coordinated but not too strongly connected writing, breadth. Rhythmic writing. Emphasis on circular movements and on horizontal connecting strokes.

(3) By the *security type* I understand the person who tries to protect himself against conflicts and their consequences, tries to avoid and to suppress them. This type covers a very wide range, from the perfectionist who wants to build himself up into a conflictless, saintly model man, down to the crook, who wears a conventional mask, and to the neurotic, who suppresses his conflicts and tries hysterically to wriggle out of them when he is faced with them and cornered.

In addition to the above, we have to subdivide the security type into the *mask type*, the *escape type*—and, as a compromise between the two, the *mimicry type*.

The mask type is a person whose protection is an artificial character, a building-up, a mask, a diplomatic approach, which, on the highest levels, becomes the model man just mentioned; on the lowest level, the discriminating criminal. The escape type is the person whose idea of self-defence is flight.

The mimicry type is the person whose self-defence is to lie flat, to imitate what he thinks are his antagonist's expectations, and who makes a constant attempt to play up to changing demands and changing environments.

The graphological indications of the mask type are: arcade

connection or copybook connection, artificial ornamental writing, initial adjustments, slow writing, covering strokes, upright or left slant, illegible writing, left moves (left tendencies), dotted writing, wide spacing between words.

The graphological indications of the escape type are: left slant or exaggerated right slant, wavy line connections, with sporadic thread connections, left moves (left tendencies), no cross strokes, or cross strokes in the wrong direction. Elliptic forms, signature to the extreme right or extreme left, broad right margin, no margin at bottom. End stroke of words suspended. Wide spacing between words.

Graphological characteristics of the mimicry type are: characterless writing, thread connection flat stroke, covering stroke, no verticality, imitative elements, especially imitations of the addressee's writing, illegibility, artificial writing, end strokes suspended, breaks, irregular spacing between words.

Most criminals and many neurotics belong to the security type.

(4) The *confused type* is a person who has an ambivalent approach to resistance, conflict and antagonism, partly facing it, partly trying to escape from it, and never able to integrate the two opposite approaches. The confused type is therefore never completely balanced or predictable in his approach. Many neurotics and psychopaths belong to the confused type.

Graphological indications of the confused type are: violent changes of angle, irregularity, breaks, especially in the signature, left as well as right tendencies, changing forms of connections, rising and falling lines, variable thickness of strokes, and shifted emphasis of pressure. Changing character of the word "I".

The writing of the conflict type will proclaim itself at first glance by its emphasis on strokes, and by its horizontal tension; the receptive type by its emphasis on circular movements; the security types by their emphasis on arcs closed at the top, or threads; and the confused type by their lack of any clear emphasis.

CHAPTER VIII

IMAGES OF THE WHOLE AND OF THE PART

I N an art exhibition you will often see not only full-size completed pictures there, but also innumerable small sketches of details from these pictures by the painter: the face, the hands of one of the people portrayed in a group, a sketch of a little dog appearing in one of the corners of a picture, or of some flowers which stand on the table.

The composition of the final picture is an image by itself, but each part of it is also a little image, complete in itself and consisting of many still smaller parts. It is the same with a handwritten manuscript.

The manuscript as a whole reflects the writer's conception of the whole, while each line, word or letter, or even part of a letter, portrays the conception which the writer has of this part. We have to realize again that all these writing images, whether whole or in part, are movement images which are executed automatically by the actual movement of creation.

There are, however, differences of emphasis between the image of the whole and of the parts which have led some theoretical graphologists, like the late Carl Gross, to divide the writing process into three elements: rhythm (individual motor impulse), which is synonymous with what we called the moving force, structure by which the execution of the guiding image of the individual letter is meant; and use of space (evenness), by which the disposition of the single elements of the manuscript on the whole sheet is meant. But Gross has to admit that the two latter elements are much interwoven; in fact, they are only two aspects of the guiding image, the image of the smaller element, the part, and the image of the whole. We have, however, to consider it both as a whole setting as well as in its elements.

When looking at a complete manuscript we have to investigate in the first line the deviation from typical forms, especially layout, distances, rhythm and configuration of the whole, the fullness of the manuscript as a whole, the treatment of intervals and the taking in or leaving out of the white space by suggestions in the strokes between words and lines, the invisible connections and proportions, the all-embracing character and subordination of the whole manuscript to a central principle.

Single words have to be examined for distance between letters and coordination between letters for legibility. It will be necessary to assess whether words are conceived and written as a clear and, at the same time, in its parts, well-balanced unit.

The basis, the unit of personal configuration and investigation will always be the single letter. This was clear in the early days of graphology and is still very much so in French graphology.

The Klages school broke away from this tradition for reasons of its own. Klages emphasized the importance of the writing as a whole of the general rhythm and evenness of the manuscript. He also investigated the general tendencies working through the whole manuscript. The more graphology became concerned with handwriting as a picture and projection of the personality as a whole, the more the movement and configuration side were studied and the more graphologists became reluctant to accept the French list of typical letter forms for certain characteristics. Handwriting is a projection of the personality as a whole, and of the writer's individual approach to particular problems of life and work.

Therefore the right way is to accept the typical forms, and at the same time to investigate the effect of all the writing tendencies on alphabet patterns, resulting in those typical deviations which are the synthesis of the different general tendencies of a writer related to an actual test situation.

I want to prove my point by demonstrating in the next chapter how any guiding image can affect any single letter of the alphabet.

CHAPTER IX

TEST SITUATIONS IN THE ALPHABET

I F we accept the fact that the guiding images of a writer are structuralizing, formative tendencies which, without his knowledge, make their mark on every single letter and stroke which he writes, the alphabet becomes a test medium, a moulding material, for the writer's sculpture, which in the end leads to a self-portrait of his personality.

Each part of the different letters will, of course, represent a different moulding influence, and each part of the letter will become a test situation for a different tendency.

In *The Graphologist's Alphabet* I have already listed the various difficulties which the shaping of each letter involves—difficulties which each writer has to solve in his own way. It is important for the student, who wants to be able to see the guiding images, to be aware of this and to watch these actual test situations in each single letter. Only this will enable him to assess the character of the structural force which drives the writer to form a particular letter in a specific way. So each particular letter in a manuscript becomes an actual synthesis of the constructive (and destructive) tendencies of the writer. In a wider field it will be also necessary to study the difficulties of connection which each combination of letters involves, in order to find out how these difficulties have been solved.

To demonstrate what the student has to learn to observe, I give here a selection of examples demonstrating how the different guiding images behind each writer exercise their structural influences on a small single letter, the letter *r*, and also how they work on connections between this letter *r* and the letter *o*.

EXAMPLE		
93		*Large*
94		*Small*
95		*Broad*
96		*Narrow*
97		*Growing and disproportionate*
98		*Diminishing and disproportionate*
99		*Rising line*
100		*Straight line*
101		*Dropping line*
102		*Upright*
103		*Slant to the right*
104		*Backward slant*

EXAMPLE

105   Right tendency

106   Left tendency

107   Direct writing

108   Roundabout writing

109   Changing angle

110   Connected and continued writing

111   Disconnected writing

112   Discontinued writing

113   Punctuated (dotted) writing

114   Rhythmic writing

115   Arrhythmic writing

116   Dislocated writing

EXAMPLE		
117		*Thick stroke*
118		*Thin stroke*
119		*Flat writing*
120		*Plastic writing*
121		*Pasty writing*
122		*Angular writing*
123		*Copy-book*
124		*Garland*
125		*Arcade*
126		*Wavy line*
127		*Thread*
128		*Regular writing*
129		*Irregular writing*

130		Enriched writing
131		Simplified writing
132		Knots
133		Overloaded writing
134		Neglected writing (garland and arcade)
135		Neglected connection
136		Full writing
137		Lean writing
138		Monotonous and discontinued writing
139		Variety of writing forms
140		Elliptic writing
141		Open writing

EXAMPLE		
142		Closed writing
143		Closed and knotted writing
144		Loops
145		Spirals
146		Square writing
147		Articulated writing
148		Unarticulated writing
149		Abnormal crossing

CHAPTER X

OTHER INFLUENCES ON HANDWRITING

THE formation of the signature is an instance of the fact that the content of the word, its emotional overtones, but also its purpose and, finally, the writer's environment, considerably influence the guiding image of writing a word.

This is, of course, not confined to the signature. It is only that an emotional view of the ego is more or less pronounced in everybody, and therefore the effect of this emotion on the writing of the symbol of the ego is obvious. Finally, the purpose of the signature is also of a common and general nature.

In the following chapters the relation between purpose, environment and content on the one side and the handwriting itself on the other will be dealt with as far as general rules can be deduced.

It is obvious that in order to analyse a handwriting successfully something should be known about the writer and about the contents of the manuscript. If this is not possible, at least a supply of writing material dating from different times and occasions is desirable for comparison. This relationship between purpose and contents on the one hand and handwriting on the other is one of the common grounds between graphology and psycho-analysis where fruitful co-operation can be established.

Before going into details, a general survey and scheme should be devised to describe the topics which have to be covered.

The purpose of a manuscript may be:

(*a*) To preserve thoughts or information for the writer's own benefit (for instance, notes).
(*b*) To copy other manuscripts.
(*c*) To pass on information (a letter, for instance).
(*d*) To impress an addressee.

In the same manuscript different parts may serve different purposes, with different emphasis; as, for instance, purely formal parts (e.g. yours sincerely), the parts which form the main contents and, finally, the address.

The environment, i.e. the writer's situation when producing the manuscript, has also to be considered from different view-points. At the moment of writing, the writer may be subject to one or more of the following influences:

(*e*) Inspiring influences.

(*f*) Distracting influences.

(*g*) Obstructive influences.

(*h*) Exciting or depressing situations.

Finally, the contents. Here we may distinguish between:

(*i*) Words which have a more or less general emotional appeal to everybody, such as figures, known names, the words "money", "you", "me", "dear", sexual expressions and special words which appeal only to very special individual complexes.

(*j*) Pleasant, inspiring and unpleasant, inhibiting contents.

(*k*) Exciting and boring contents.

As to the graphic effects of these different stimuli, we have to list:

(*l*) Making the writing more remarkable, or making it more unobtrusive.

(*m*) An accelerating or loosening, or retarding or inhibiting effect.

(*n*) The subjection of the writing to the influence of will and control, or of fears.

(*o*) Making the writing clearer or more illegible.

(*p*) Making the writing artificial or disguised.

(*q*) Imitative effects.

(*r*) Deliberate writing mistakes or disintegration of the writing.

(*s*) Causing amendments.

According to this scheme let us investigate in the next few chapters the different influences and their effects under the following headlines:

(i) Official and unofficial writing.

(ii) The address and the addressee.

(iii) Emotion and environment.

(iv) The contents of the manuscript.

(v) Writing mistakes and amendments.

(vi) Changes and developments in the guiding image.

(vii) The central core of the writing.

CHAPTER XI

OFFICIAL AND UNOFFICIAL WRITING

IN most cases notes merely designed to preserve for the writer himself thoughts, dates or information are written in a slightly different way from letters and other manuscripts whose purpose it is to pass on information or something else to a third person.

In his notebook the writer is at home, is not formally dressed. He writes as it were in his shirt-sleeves. In a letter or any other manuscript written for other people's use or inspection, the writer is in a more official capacity. Even this official character changes in degree between manuscripts for entirely official use, such as application forms, and private letters sent to friends or members of the family. We have already mentioned when discussing signatures that some people in the public eye have a different signature when they write to their wives from when they sign a document.

To a certain degree these differences between official and unofficial writing are justified by the purpose, as is the informality of the man at leisure in his own home and the formality of the man in an office or in an official capacity.

It is, for instance, a question of importance for the addressee that any manuscript intended for him should be legible to him; but it is sometimes the intention of a writer of notes to keep his thoughts to himself. We know, for example, that Leonardo da Vinci, who wanted to keep his inventions secret, learnt a "mirror-writing". Furthermore, most communications intended for others have to comply with a certain habitual form, have to be signed and composed in an intelligible style and layout, while notes can be abbreviated and written in haste, in slogans or in some other private shorthand.

Manuscripts designed for others have also to be fitted into standardized types of letter sheets, postcards, etc., while notes can be done in any form with any writing instrument on any slip of paper. Notes can be written in fits and starts, while it is usual to conceive a letter as a whole and then to write it all at one go.

Finally, there are differing degrees of interest in the contents.

All these circumstances make a comparison between manuscripts of a private and of an official character by the same writer interesting. If official and private manuscripts are written in the same way it shows that the writer does not change his behaviour, whether he is alone and unobserved or watched by others; that he behaves just in the same way when he is with others as when alone. This becomes particularly interesting when either the writing is very neglected or when it is exceptionally accurate, regular or stylized, ornamented and complicated.

A writer who writes his letters in the same slipshod fashion as his notes is a man who does not mind sitting in his office in underwear and dressing-gown. He does not care about the effect on others; he does not tidy up when things become "official". The person, on the other hand, who writes his notes as carefully and regularly as his letters possesses an almost pedantic accuracy. He is a person who always wears his best clothes, whether he is in his office or at home. If the writing is stylized, complicated or ornamental it belongs to a writer who is keen on impressing others all the time.

The main interest in comparison is, however, the difference in the actual handwriting employed for official and private purposes. If this difference is merely a matter of the writing becoming more regular, better articulated, slower and more upright, then it just shows that the writer is aware that he has to be more considerate or more cautious when dealing with others. But when the discrepancy between the two manuscripts is more marked, then we can deduce that the guiding images of the writer's official and of his private personality are different; that he has, so to speak, an official face and a private face, that he is writing-conscious and wants to evoke reactions and make impressions which are tied up with his public personality and have nothing to do with his private ego.

In these cases it is interesting to investigate which features of his own character the writer officially emphasizes; whether, for instance, he writes larger because he wants to emphasize his personal importance; whether he writes more fully and more ornamentally in order to emphasize imagination and artistic interests; or whether he writes slanting to the right in order to emphasize his sociability.

There are also cases where the normal writing shows discrepancies in angle or directions of lines. If one wants to find out which of these contrasting features belong to the private and which to the official person it is helpful to look at notes on the one hand and at some official bits of writing on the other.

One of the most official forms of writing is the address on the envelope. I suggest dealing with this in the next chapter.

CHAPTER XII

THE ADDRESS AND THE ADDRESSEE

NOTHING, no other part of a letter, is so distinctly governed by a purpose as the address on the envelope. It is, in essence, nothing else than an order to the post office to deliver the letter to a person whose name and domicile are displayed on the envelope in a conventional, easily grasped form. This involves two elements: clarity and regularity, in order to enable the post-office officials to read it. Clever display in order to enable the essentials to be taken in at a quick glance and, as part of that, sticking to the display conventions of a particular country which conduce to this quick grasp. A writer who renounces one of these elements, i.e. who either writes unintelligibly or tries to avoid display (for instance, by writing too small) or who avoids the orthodox distribution of the name and living-place on the cover, shows that he puts his personal preferences and idiosyncracies higher than the demands of an ordinary and commonly accepted purpose; he also displays lack of consideration for others.

The motives of this unorthodoxy may, however, be different in the cases mentioned. In the case of the person who writes unintelligibly (Example 150) the reason is that his emotional complexity, or his preoccupation with what is inside the letter, prevents the writing being intelligible to others, and does not take into account other people's justified claims to serve the common purpose best; in the second case, where the writer avoids display (Example 151) an extreme dislike of any public display, of any self-dramatization, may be the reason. The third case (Example 152) is the work of a writer who either from rebellious instincts or from vanity wants to be unorthodox. All these three types of writing an address will, however, have one thing in common: that their authors are either unable or unwilling to perform a public function which involves some display, and that they are especially unable or unwilling to consider or to accept a generally accepted common purpose.

This leads to the second important contribution which an address has to make to graphological investigation, the difference between "private" writing and writing for public display. Much has already been said about this difference between the man in private, the private ego and the public man, the public ego, how these two compare and what insight into the writer's personality can be gained by comparing these two aspects of him. What makes the address so important in this connection is that it is the most outspoken and clear-cut of all pieces of public writing.

There is another more technical aspect of this. To suit the purpose of the address it has in many cases to be written bigger and more slowly than the text. This helps us to see to what extent an individual can change the size of his writing, and what other changes this alteration involves. It will also show the differences between his quicker and his slower style of writing.

EXAMPLE 150
Unintelligible address. Emotional complexity, lack of consideration

EXAMPLE 151
Dislike of public display and of self-dramatization

EXAMPLE 152
Freakish unorthodoxy of distribution

The third interesting aspect of the written address is the distribution of its parts on the envelope. The essential parts of it are: the name of the addressee; the place, consisting of house number, street name and town name (John Smith, 3 Cambridge Road, Liverpool). To these often have to be added: an indication of sex and title (Sir, Dr., Esq., Miss or Mrs., Mr., Messrs.), the name of a county or district (Hertfordshire), the name of a country (Switzerland), and, in some cases, the name of the house (Robin's Nest).

The usual distribution is started either with the title (Sir, Messrs.) in the first line, or all these connected with a name in the same line (Messrs. Lilac Press Ltd). If the title (Messrs.) stands alone, the name forms a second line. Then comes house number and street (third line), then the name of the town (fourth line), followed by the name of the district (fifth line), or the name of the country (fifth line or placed separately on the left-hand side).

The title is usually placed slightly to the left, the name more or less in the centre, the place to the right.

The arrangement and placing of these parts by an individual writer allows for several potentialities which all have their own significance. Each of these preferences mentioned has its special meaning (Example 153).

(1) Emphasis on the left-hand side indicates a general reluctance to get out of oneself, a clinging to security, a readiness to run away from difficult situations.

(2) Emphasis on the upper part adds an element of dreaminess, of being up in the air (Example 154).

(3) Emphasis on the lower part adds an element of materialism and depression (Example 155).

(4) Emphasis on the centre reveals concentration, purposefulness and skill in putting ideas into action, but also at the same time a certain carefulness about husbanding one's strength (Example 156).

(5) General emphasis on the right side puts social and general considerations first (Example 157).

(6) Emphasis on the lower parts adds an element of materialism and depression (Example 158).

(7) Distribution all over the envelope originates from a desire to preserve unbroken continuity of effort (Example 159).

Dr Eric Singer

2·9 Abercorn place

London N. W. 8

EXAMPLE 153
General emphasis on the left-hand side of the envelope

Dr Eric Singer

2 9 Abercorn place

London N. W. 8

EXAMPLE 154
Emphasis on the upper part of the left-hand side

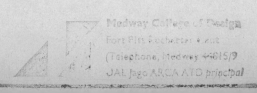

EXAMPLE 155
Emphasis on the lower part of the left-hand side

EXAMPLE 156
Emphasis on the centre

EXAMPLE 157
General emphasis on the right-hand side

EXAMPLE 158
Emphasis on the lower part of the right-hand side

EXAMPLE 159
Distribution all over the envelope

Max Pulver, who, with another Swiss, Max Keller, has done most of the more recent investigations into addresses—his work being preceded by the findings of the French research workers Aruss and Duparchy Jeannez—sees in a handwriting which develops like a ladder from left to right (Example 159) an indication of caution and distrust, of making contact bit by bit only.

The distribution on the envelope will also have to be watched for skilful use of space or otherwise, showing whether the writer has a quick grasp of the possibilities of correct exploitation of space and of his available opportunities.

One more point of interest in addresses is that most of the words of which an address is made up have potentially a strong emotional appeal to the writer. Titles, figures, places, towns and countries, all affect our imaginations, and may produce a positive loosening or a negative inhibiting, even irritating effect on the writer which may well express itself as emphasis, neglect, or even mistakes and amendments, when writing the word concerned. So, of course, will in some cases the name of the addressee. This does not apply to the address only. We have to realize that every letter written to another person is, in fact, an imagined dialogue with this person. Although not actively involved in the job of writing the letter, the addressee is to a larger or smaller degree present in the mind of the writer, who is especially reminded of his opposite number when he has to write his name or words like "Dear", "you", "Sincerely", etc.

This imagined presence of the addressee, this radiation of his hetero-ego, of his personality as seen and experienced by the writer, often has very striking effects on the shape and character of single words, or even of the whole writing. One day a man sent me about twelve different examples of his writing style which, although they were of course similar in basic trends, all looked different. (I have reproduced some of these manuscripts as Quiz No. 10 in my *Quiz Book*.) This gentleman wrote me that whenever he had to answer a letter he could not help adapting his writing to an imitation of the style of writing of his addressee, and asked me how I could explain his being influenced by the addressees in this way. It is, of course, a not unknown phenomenon. My own wife, for instance, when she speaks on the phone to anyone with a noticeably unusual accent, tends to adopt this accent in her own speech. I can always tell without asking her when she is speaking to a Hungarian or a Prussian. This unconscious imitation is, to a certain extent, present in everybody, and forms the basis of our understanding of other personalities.

The actor who today plays Caesar and tomorrow Hamlet, the comedian who parodies the intonation of a voice, and in this way takes on the character of another man, the child who laughs if you laugh, the hypnotized crowd, who repeat the slogans of a demagogue, they all follow the law of unconscious imitation.

As has been explained in Chapter III, it is also one of the roots of graphological understanding of a writer's character. Experiments with hypnosis, conducted by Professor Preyer and others, have shown that hypnotized persons adopt in their writing the characters suggested to them, that they scribble like children when told they are children, and write with a flourish when told they are Napoleon. But how, apart from these extreme cases of imitation, can an addressee influence the writing of a letter? In many cases, not at all, because the emotional outlet will either be in the text of the letter or not present at all in the letter in question. But often it may influence the writing as a whole, or at least the individual words of stronger emotional content, like the name, the "dear", etc., as already mentioned.

In one case I had the opportunity of comparing the signature of a man in his notebooks with the writing of the same man in some letters which he wrote to his principal competitor and successful rival. While his notebook signature was—although underlined, and with emphasis on the capital letters—very small, the writing in the letters to his rival was four times as large, the signature nearly five times as large. As I knew that this man, who had very little real self-assertion, always began to boast, sometimes actually to lie when speaking to his competitor, whom he wanted to impress and beside whom he wished to make a good show, the two writings gave a very correct picture of the relations between the two men. This was again one of those cases where a certain knowledge of personal relations and an ample choice of writing material for investigation is necessary and where only a combination of the graphological technique with the psychoanalytical could give the best results.

In general it can be said that a positive reaction to the addressee will increase the size of the words referring to him while a negative one will inhibit and reduce the writing of these words and enlarge in comparison the ego-symbols which help self-assertion.

CHAPTER XIII

CIRCUMSTANCES, ENVIRONMENT, PHYSICAL CONDITIONS AND MOODS

WE have said that environment and moods may influence a particular piece of handwriting. Environment in three possible ways: by distracting the writer's attention, and in this way making his writing more distracted (disconnected), or by subjecting the writer to some shock, also resulting in breaks. Writing circumstances of a technical or of a climatic nature may also affect the writing. The first—for instance, writing in a moving train—may result in changing the firmness of the stroke or the direction of the line; the second, like moods or physical conditions, may make the writing more lethargic or more free and easy.

Environment may affect not only a particular manuscript, but, in the long run, by furnishing new visual impressions to a person, may induce him to integrate some of these new impressions into his writing style, of course without altering the basic features of this style, the particular graphic formula of his personality. It may enrich the writer's scope, without altering his forming principles. In the chapter on pictorial writing, cases of this impact of visual impressions originating from environment have been mentioned.

Saudek, who compared writings of blind persons with those of writers with normal sight, found that the writing of blind men tended to become more stationary owing to the missing influence of outward impressions.

As to moods, which we may define as different states of readiness to meet and to integrate outward experiences (and, we can include, with moods, physical illness and intoxication), they may show in the handwriting—just as they show more crudely in the writing of manic-depressive types: high spirits by extension in size and breadth and by rising lines; depression by becoming smaller, narrower and by descending lines. Other changes of mood, such as sudden excitement or an outburst of temper, may show in a decline of regularity, irregular and accentuated pressure or in trembling strokes. I may here refer to the specimen of Dr. Clement's farewell letter in *Graphology for Everyman*, which shows the effect of intoxication as well as of a very unusual and depressed state of mind in the writing. Nevertheless, the letter forms are not much impaired, and the characteristic inner laws and proportions remain intact.

This is confirmed (Examples 160, 161) by many investigations made on people in different states of mind, different circumstances and environment and different physical conditions. Jacoby collected the handwritings of dying people. Lombroso gives examples of the handwriting of people before and after epileptic attacks.

EXAMPLE 160

EXAMPLE 161

The signature of the Hungarian Cardinal Mindszenty in normal times (Example 160) and during his trial after "confessions" had been obtained from him (Example 161). The second example shows trembling features, reduced breadth, omissions, irregularities, breaks and disconnections. But the basic character of this disintegrating writing still remains the same: forward slant, thin stroke, regularity of style and breadth, narrowness, garland connection, proportions, covering strokes, diminishing size, forms of letters.

That faulty conclusions can be drawn from the fact that the handwriting remains basically unaffected by all these influences was demonstrated to me by the late Professor Joad, who on the B.B.C. Brains Trust was once asked what he thought of graphology. Joad answered that he had made one investigation on his own by comparing the handwriting of a famous historical person at normal times with his signature when he was in prison before his execution. As Joad could not see the slightest difference he concluded that there could be hardly anything in character-reading from handwriting. He failed to see that the fact that handwriting remains basically unaffected by moods and circumstances—just like the basic character of personality—is the strongest argument in favour of graphology.

So the only cases where a real change of the appearance of handwriting occurs should be those when personality changes. I deal with that in the next chapter.

CHAPTER XIV

INFLUENCE OF THE SUBJECT-MATTER

IT is, of course, not only the ego-symbols and words relating to the addressee which may rouse the writer's emotional associations. I have already mentioned some others, such as figures or the word "money". There are many more which involve a typical complex of associations, a complex which is easily accessible to interpretation and will evoke more or less identical associations in different people, though the impact of these associations may most strongly affect a writer who has some unconscious fixation and complexes ready to be released by the image of the provoking word. Here are a few such words: death, grave, knife, gun, suicide, cruelty, prison, mother, father, brother, sister, crime, marriage, wife, child, illness, and, of course, names of persons, towns, countries and of certain diseases.

I found two very clear examples of the effect of names on the writer in two more recent criminal cases. One is the farewell letter of Dr. Clements, the Southport poisoner, reproduced in my book, *Graphology for Everyman*. This letter, written after the writer had taken a deadly poison, is a revealing document of self-destruction and disintegration, with drooping lines. Only one line rises. This is the one line where are mentioned the names of the friends who have stuck by him and on whom his last friendly thoughts are centred. Another uncanny example is a letter written by John Christie the murderer to his wife's family, where he writes on behalf of his murdered spouse, pretending that she is too ill to write herself: when he comes to write down her name the inhibiting elements radiating from this name become so strong that he makes a mistake and has to amend his writing.

These are all typical effects, and while the specific complex and fixation affected by the word may still have to be defined by psychoanalysis, the graphologist can remark the potential existence of such a complex.

It is more difficult with other words of a less typical, less generally evocative character, but which still, because of their completely different handling by the writer, arouse the graphologist's suspicions.

Different parts of the body, nose, ear, legs, may have fairly easily traceable relations to the writer's emotional difficulties; but there are other, generally completely unsuspected words—as psycho-analysis has so convincingly brought out—which may provoke the unconscious fixations of the writer, just as a smell or a flower sometimes suddenly bring back to us far-off, remote memories of our youth.

As psycho-analysis, especially the analysis of dreams, has proved, the connection with a complex is sometimes very indirect, masked, distorted and hidden. It is the business of the analyst to trace the exact connection; graphology can do no more than point to the existence of an anomaly, and leave it to the analyst to find out what it means.

The character of a handwriting is sometimes affected not by single words but by the general contents of the letter or another manuscript. A pupil of mine once showed me two different letters by the same writer, written within a week of each other, both on the same size notepaper. The writing of the second, although the letter was no longer than the first, was just half the size. It was clearly the contents of the second letter which had this contracting effect on the writer's mood. In the first letter he had invited my pupil out for the evening, in the second he apologized for not being able to keep the appointment. This unconscious effect of an unpleasant content on the character of the writing (or of an interesting, pleasant, boring, irrelevant, exciting, aggressive content) is sometimes very different from the effect which a conscious effort connected with the contents may produce.

How he reacts to a certain content will also depend on the individual temperament of the writer. A boring content, for instance, may induce one child to write more slowly because of failing initiative, another to write larger in order to write less and still to fill the space, another to write smaller for the same reason as the writer of the apologetic letter, another to write more quickly in a desperate attempt to get over it.

Here again, if, by comparison of two letters, the graphologist finds a striking discrepancy of size, breadth, speed, direction of lines or writing mistakes in the course of a single letter, the content may throw light on the reason, or may at least be a hint to find out by analysis what there was in the contents which influenced the writer. It was Freud who first pointed to the anomalies which might be found in everyday actions, like mistakes of speech, faults of memory and writing mistakes.

From the graphological point of view, the meaning of mis-spelling and other writing mistakes and of amendments has been partially investigated by analytically minded or trained grapho-logical research workers like Pulver, Saudek, Werner Wolff and Daim. It has also been extensively dealt with by psychiatrists investigating the handwriting of mentally sick persons—such as Lombroso, Bleuler, Rogues de Fursac and many others.

It seems to me worth while to devote a separate chapter to this question of writing mistakes, misspelling and amendments.

EXAMPLE 162
Part of first "n" omitted

EXAMPLE 163
Repetition of part of second "n"

EXAMPLE 164
Contamination ("d" and "n" change places)

EXAMPLE 165
Amendment ("o" retraced)

CHAPTER XV

WRITING MISTAKES AND AMENDMENTS

THERE are five distinct forms of writing mistakes:

(1) Omissions of letters, parts of letters, or whole words (Example 162).

(2) Repetitions of letter, parts of letters, or whole words (Example 163).

(3) Contamination (which means that the sequence of letters, parts of letters, or words is changed). Contractions fall under the heading of contamination (Example 164).

(4) Retouching, retracing, amendments (Example 165).

(5) Unconscious substitution of one word for another.

For these writing mistakes there are different reasons.

(a) General physiological or psychological reasons, such as a general irritation, sometimes from physical, sometimes from psychological causes.

(b) Special psychological reasons (complexes, fixations) connected with the sound, the visual or phonetic associations, or the meaning of words.

(c) Extreme desire for perfection.

(d) A mental defect which makes the writer unable to advance his thoughts logically, interferes with his memory and his coordination of thought, and destroys the coherence of his guiding images.

Let us now deal with these five forms of writing mistakes one by one. They have been investigated by research workers of very different views. Among the earlier investigators, Meier and Meringer (a philologist and a psychiatrist) described and differentiated various errors in speaking which are also interesting for the study of writing mistakes. Then Freud made his sensational discoveries of the hidden and unconscious meaning of these little mistakes and of their complex character (*die Fehlleistungen*). Professor Bleuler of Zurich, in his universally recognized textbook on psychiatry, paid great attention to the different forms of writing mistakes characteristic of different mental diseases. Among graphologists it was mainly Saudek who studied the subject.

Omissions are the most frequent and also the most harmless form of writing mistakes. Some are intentional, like the omission of certain letters in a stylized signature. In hastily written notes, or in abbreviations following a dictation, the shorthand character of this quick type of writing, which becomes purely speed and touch writing, almost without visual control, is most likely to lead to frequent omissions. In any first draft of a difficult manuscript, or one written in a foreign language, where the writer's concentration on the context is much greater than usual, such writing mistakes are merely an indication of over-concentration, which inhibits and hampers the easy automatic flow of writing images and causes these omissions. It seems to me, however, that not enough attention has been paid to the difference in omissions by different writers. There is, as Meier and Meringer correctly said, a different evaluation and validity of the different sounds of a word in each writer's mind, and applied to writing there must also be a different evaluation of the picture of individual letters. We know that in some Oriental languages the consonants are quite differently treated from the majority of vowels, and form the skeleton of writing and printing. The visual type of writer will, when haste, strain or fatigue irritates him, still tend to keep the visual skeleton of his writing intact and rather omit vowels than consonants. The aural type of writer will rather tend to phonetic spelling and there rather omit consonants than vowels. The word "psychiatry" will, as a skeleton word, look like "pschtry" to the visual, but sound like "chiary" to the phonetic type of writer.

We will have to interpret omissions in cases of great speed or great mental strain as natural consequences of a higher degree of concentration on some aspects of the manuscript's contents, upsetting and irritating the automatic reproduction of the guiding image; when we examine what has been left out, we can decide whether the writer belongs to the visual or the aural type. Absence of omissions and lack of irritation in an example of very quick writing or in a very difficult draft may be taken as proof of a well-balanced, sound mind and memory.

Frequent omissions in normal manuscripts—normal speed, not too difficult contents—are, however, a sign of great irritation.

Mental strain, nervous weakness, physical tiredness, exhaustion or intoxication, strong distracting influences of environment, compulsion to write under unusual circumstances, are comparatively harmless reasons for frequent omissions; mental illness or loss of memory, more dangerous. This applies not only to the omission of letters or parts of words, but also to the omission of whole words. Here, of course, the Freudian explanation of a complex connected with the word (real contents or phonetic association), accompanied by a desire to suppress the associations connected with that word, is a potential reason for leaving it out.

While omissions come from a blurring, inaccuracy and uncertainty of the movement picture guiding the automatic flow of the hand, because of the highly strung, overstrained working of the whole writing apparatus, repetitions—or, as Saudek calls them, perseverations—come from a failure of control in the writing movement. Counter-checks no longer regulate the flow of meaningless, automatic movements in favour of the directed, purposeful, singular move. There is a failure of will and control which allows the moving hand to go on while the intended image has already been fixed on the paper. The degree of irritation which this mistake indicates ranges from strong distraction, nervous irritation, physical strain and exhaustion, etc., to complexes involved in repeated words. But here we also find the uncanny repetitions of the same word or letter—the so-called verbigerations—characteristic of the writing of persons suffering from mental diseases of the katatonic type: a stereotyped monotony corresponding to the same stereotyped monotony in their speech, gestures and posture, a writing which reminds you of a broken gramophone record monotonously and meaninglessly repeating the same sounds.

By "contamination" I mean a change in the sequence of letters of a word, for instance, writing *wiht* instead of *with*. This would be called an anticipation, because the second letter *h* changes place with the first letter *t*.

If a former letter is repeated, as, for instance, if somebody writes *instsance* instead of *instance*, we speak of a resonance, because this repetition is due to the resonance of the previous *s* in the writer's mind.

A third form of contamination is the contraction of two words into a single word, as, for instance, *twwords* instead of *two words*.

While anticipations almost always point to impatience or boredom, or the desire to finish the writing of a word in a hurry, contractions should always be examined for the phonetic associations which they may contain and which may point to a suppressed word, a Freudian complex. Apart from that, contamination is just a nervous or physical irritation of different degree in different writers.

Retracing, amending or retouching a word or letter already written may be done for various reasons. The most common and plausible one is to embellish, to correct spelling mistakes, or to make a word more legible. This is a legitimate reason and not much importance need be attached to it. It must, however, be judged differently if writing mistakes of the types (*a*) to (*c*) are retraced and corrected afterwards. Here the writing mistake (*a*) to (*c*) is the primary thing and has to be taken into account in the way just explained.

But there are cases of retracing where neither the legibility nor a previous mistake is the cause of the amendment and the retracing is done without obvious reasons. This may be either caused by a shock effect of the retraced word in the Freudian sense, like the retracing of his wife's name in Mr. Christie's letter, or it may originate from an extreme desire for perfection. This writer is the type of man who cannot leave things alone when they are finished, out of a neurotic uncertainty and fear.

It may sometimes be interesting to examine what has been retraced in order to get an idea what forms the writer wanted to suppress and what he liked to substitute for them, following the general lines of graphological interpretation.

The replacement of one word by another word with a different and often opposite meaning is what Freud really was after. Here a suppressed intention is represented by the word written in error, which contradicts the word the writer consciously wanted to write. Freud gives the famous example of a poisoner who asked in a letter for some poison to try it out on mice and instead of "mice" unconsciously wrote "men", thus unconsciously disclosing his sinister intentions. Often a phonetic or visual likeness between the two words leads to the association which finally produces the mistake.

CHAPTER XVI

CHANGES OF PERSONALITY IN HANDWRITING

PERSONALITY develops from the day of birth onwards, and so does handwriting, which faithfully registers this development. If the character of the personality changes considerably or completely, the handwriting changes accordingly. Sometimes it takes time for the development or change of character to become obvious in the handwriting and for what remains of the old routine to be replaced by new writing features. Sometimes changes in handwriting are like a red light warning of imminent changes of character long before these changes have become obvious to those who know the writer. But in the end the correlation between handwriting and the personality of the writer becomes obvious.

Many investigations have been made to this effect. The hypnotic experiments of Professor Preyer, who suggested to hypnotized subjects that they were emperors or children, proved that with a different conception of their personality their writing changed accordingly: that these persons wrote in a stilted way when they thought they were royalties or dictators; and in a childish way when they believed they were infants.

Other research workers have collected handwritings of persons before and after an obvious change of personality had taken place in the writers, and compared them. For instance, before and after psychoanalysis, or—as Jacoby did—before and after religious conversion, which in most cases made the handwriting simpler and more humble.

The development of the writing of children or of adults right through their lives has also been studied. Saudek, in an article on the development of a public schoolboy published in his paper *Personality*, analysed eighty-one letters written by a boy from his first day at school until after puberty.

To be able to analyse the corresponding changes and development of handwriting systematically and scientifically, some consideration must first be given to what is meant by personality, by development, and by change. Here we have to go back to some of my earlier statements in previous chapters. In chapter II I explained that the process of writing is put into motion according to a forming principle (the guiding image) by a motor impulse (the moving force). These two factors together form the focus and spirit of each personality. They take account of both the outside world and the subject's inner development, the physical and social influences at work upon him.

The guiding image, the forming principles (which also corresponds to Freud's *Id*, to Aristotle's *Entelecheia*, to Socrates' Daemon, to the personal God, to the soul, etc.), structurizes impressions, associations, projects and expressions of the human person, while the moving force furnishes the energy behind the guiding image, keeps these various items in balance and keeps them going, translates them into action (of which writing is one).

We have to remember that, while based on the body-mind unit of an individual person, this structural pattern and structurizing force forms a unit. This unit is only loosely knit and of an elastic and contrasting pattern and sometimes (remember the confused type of writing) a unit full of discrepancy, where forces and counter-forces are balanced with difficulty.

Three more factors have to be kept in mind:

(i) Differences in the physical basis and changes in this basis, beginning with growing to maturity and ending with physical decay.

(ii) Differences in the formative material, personal encounters, experiences, impressions, problems, environment and achievement.

(iii) The fact that conception of personality often embraces two egos—one unknown to others, the private ego, *l'homme dedans*, and the other, the official ego, the hetero-ego, *l'homme dehors*, the public figure.

Only when we keep all these factors of personality in mind are we able to assess them properly and to follow up their registration in handwriting samples.

Let us sum it up in the following way:

(1) PHYSICAL BASIS OF PERSONALITY

(*a*) General development and changes: (i) growing up to maturity; (ii) decay in old age.

(*b*) Incidental development: changes caused by illness or accidents.

(2) GUIDING IMAGE AND MOVING FORCE

(*c*) Shifting emphasis on individual trends (for instance, changes in emphasis on either form, continuity or direction).

(*d*) Difference in balance of contrasting images (stronger tension between contrasting tendencies, weakening of general balance and integrating strength. Suppression of one image by another).

(3) EXPERIENCES AND ENCOUNTERS. MATERIAL FOR EXPRESSION AND
　　IMPRESSION

(*e*) Material getting richer or poorer (too few or too many impressions).

(*f*) Material changing (civilian becomes soldier).

(*g*) Integration, suppression or rejection of this experience.

(4) EGO AND HETERO-EGO

(*h*) Shift of emphasis to the private ego.

(*i*) Shift of emphasis to the official ego.

Only by keeping this scheme in mind shall we be able to see what part of the personality has undergone development or change; to what degree they have become integrated into the whole personality and to what degree the original guiding and structurizing patterns and forces are still present.

Let me give some examples. If a young man of twenty, who has up to that age written with a backward slant, then starts to write with a forward slant we may be justified in saying that he was able to sever the attachments that held him to his childhood and early days, and that his attitude to life has now become more extroverted.

If a woman, after the birth of her first child, writes in a fuller and broader style, we may be right in saying that her life has been enriched by the experience of becoming a mother. If a careerist changes his signature into an illegible "official stamp", and his handwriting into an artificial style, we may assume that the public figure has swallowed up the private man. If a subject changes the copybook style of his writing we may assume that he desires to make a change in his style of life.

One question still remains open. Are there cases where the personality (and consequently the writing) changes completely? Answered without pedantry, there are four cases which come very near to it, or can even be regarded as complete changes:

(*a*) Complete artificiality. If a person becomes so involved in his hetero-ego that it swallows up his whole private life, his writing becomes more and more artificial so that the official man entirely replaces the private one. This is not a real substitution, but a super-imposition which still leaves some connection and integration with the former state, so that the underlying personality and the structurizing principle can still be exposed, although some of the guiding images have suppressed the others.

Even in the writing of hypnotized persons these basic principles may be traced. But there are other cases where the image becomes so strong that the writer becomes mentally ill, thinking that he is God, Napoleon, a ghost or a horse. These cases give rise to extraordinary-looking writings, from the one-man's alphabet to the excessive exaggerations of one trend. There are also stereotyped repetitions and word-groups which you find in most collections of writing of mentally ill persons and in textbooks on psychiatry, notably those by the Italian professor, Lombroso, the Swiss professor, Bleuler, and the French professor, Rogues de Fursac.

Stereotyped repetitions are specially interesting because they have become gestures without meaning, very similar to the physical postures and gestures of the writers. Will, action and movement have become completely detached from intention and control, and go on automatically, like cracked gramophone records.

(*b*) Decay of the personality may be the result of physical as well as mental causes. The stereotyped features mentioned above are just a mask behind which decay has developed. In some other cases the disintegration of the personality is reflected in a complete decay, degeneration and lack of coherence in the writing: breaks, omissions, lack of continuation and proportion, degeneration of the stroke into bare threads, etc.

(*c*) The lost personality—somebody who forgets his whole personality and lives a completely different life for a time, until he

returns to his former ego—is one of the rarest and most peculiar
cases known to psychology. Bleuler records that in some extremely
rare cases one person lived not only two, but more lives; in one
known case, twelve different lives.

Working on the findings of modern psychology from Freud to
Bleuler, from Kraepelin to Jung, we can attribute these and most
other changes of personality, including hypnosis and different sorts
of influences and suggestions, to some such cause as this. As
personality is, in varying degrees, of an ambivalent nature, with
contrasting and multiple images, only balanced and harmonized
by a loose and elastic selecting and integrating principle, by a
personal force of rhythm; and, as not all experiences are properly
integrated, but some are suppressed, there is a latent readiness for
change, for sets of associations and images of a different layer,
which sometimes respond to suggestions, inspiring experiences,
influences and encounters, and then suddenly break out.

The handwriting of a lost personality, in its different existences,
can be a very interesting study. Unfortunately, I could not trace
this rare material.

(*d*) While the *lost* personality changes its character ultimately,
the *split* personality shows two characters at the same time.
Schizophrenia, the pathological splitting of personality, is the
most obvious case. Graphology, as Klages emphasizes, has not
yet been able to demonstrate one clear feature common to all
people suffering from schizophrenia. But all strikingly sudden
and abrupt changes in a handwriting point to strongly contrasting
schizoid trends. The latest investigations by the Dutch graphologist, Brail, have found that statistically the most frequent
characteristic of people who according to the medical records
suffer from schizophrenia is a sudden and unrhythmical discrepancy between an exaggeratedly thin and an exaggeratedly thick
stroke (Examples 166, 167).

EXAMPLES 166 AND 167
Pathological alterations between very thin and very thick strokes

CHAPTER XVII

THE COLOUR OF WRITING AND SHADES
OF THE STROKE

THIS study of the guiding image as the core of personality and of its expression in handwriting would not be complete without a chapter on the colour of writing; on the deliberate but still unconscious preference which a writer expresses when he chooses ink of a certain colour as his favourite medium for writing. It is, of course, not true that a person always *chooses* his pen and ink. The post-office pen would, otherwise, hardly ever be used.

In the long run everybody finds out and habitually uses the pen which he thinks fits his hand, his particular sense of grip, touch and resistance, and an ink which suits his taste. The choice lies between blue and black, in all their shades and combinations, including a greyish-black shade, between violet, green, brown and red.

There has been little study of the subject in the past on the part of graphologists, although the early writers drew attention to the general implications of the choice. Rudolphine Poppee, clever and experienced Austrian graphologist, in particular has made a detailed study of this subject. Among contemporary research workers, Johannes Pulver, Max Pulver's son, has devoted his first work to the topic (which book has unfortunately not been available to me).

Recent research in medical psychology has stressed the existence of sympathy and antipathy to certain colours and the Rohrschach tests make ample use of it. All these results should prove useful to the graphologist as well.

I have not found time yet to make a special investigation into the subject, and can therefore only repeat here what is known to me as traditional common ground in earlier graphological observation, and from my own experience and limited knowledge of the new lines of research.

First of all we have to distinguish between people who have a strong sense of colour and like loud colours, and those who like pale, watered colours. Poppee first pointed out that painters and all people who like strong and lively colours write with a strongly coloured stroke, while people who like a life and background of pastel shades or water-colours prefer to produce this impression by their strokes. Here, however, a further distinction has to be made, which Mrs. Poppee did not elaborate, namely, between people who like water-colours and those who do not like colours at all, or are afraid of them. While, in the first case, although the colours are bright, light and soft, the stroke is still broad and colourful, in the second case the stroke is reduced to a thin colourless line. I may add that the lovers of strong colours will probably choose the darker shades, intense black, black and dark blue, while the lovers of water-colours will resort to the softer shades, pale greyish-black and soft, bright blue. Another observation of Mrs. Poppee's can be fully confirmed: a combination of strongly coloured writing with tasteless and exaggerated forms of letters is indicative of a vulgar and obtrusive taste and of self-advertisement.

Another observation of Mrs. Poppee's, however, needs careful elaboration: if basically fine and thin writing alternates with strong, thick, colourful strokes, Mrs. Poppee explains it by sudden changes from a preference for soft water-colours to one for strong colours. This may be so, but these observations give only the facts and not the psychological background with which we have to deal as well.

An investigation of these matters is, today, able to draw not only on the general principles of graphological explanation, on some highly specialized investigations of medical graphology—as, for instance, the very interesting study of H. Brail on the handwriting of schizophrenics and other psychopathic writers—on the very important investigations on the character of the stroke by Hartge, Wieser, Hegar and Pophal, but also on the observations of colour-psychology, especially applied to the Rohrschach test. The common denotations of language and mythology in respect of colours will also be of some help.

First, colours. The Rohrschach test, which confronts the subject with a series of ink-blots, and draws conclusions from their answers to the question as to what associations these ink-blots awake in them, uses black, two-coloured and multi-coloured ink-blots as well. According to Rohrschach, the absence of any reference to colours in the answers reveals a lack of relationship to the outer world. Colours have a strong evocative appeal, and the absence of reaction to this appeal reveals the already-mentioned lack of relationship to the stimuli of the outer world, sometimes even lack of sentiment, or even a neurotic fear of the more colourful aspects of life. If we accept this theory and use it for graphological purposes, we have to start with the general statement that the writer who uses a certain colour wants to use it in order to create a certain impression. Colourful impressions, therefore, are intended to make a strong impact on the outer world, to create sentiment and, in extreme cases, shock and fear.

Of the colours used in handwriting (black, grey, blue, green, violet and red), red is the one likely to create the strongest shock. In mythology and in popular belief, red is the colour of passion, of fire, of blood, of Satan and of the robes of power. From the professional point of view, the king's robes, of the prosecuting attorney in the law courts, of the hangman, the marks of the censor, the corrections of a schoolmaster or accountant are all red. The flag of revolution and revolutionary parties is a red flag. The red light at the street crossing is a danger sign. The red lantern was the trade sign of the brothels. But the Red Cross is also the appeal to warriors to respect the bearers of this sign of a humanistic institution. The use of the colour red in writing may have something to do with one of these interpretations: the shock effect, the passion, which may even lead to crime, or censorship, schoolmasterly supervision, and prosecuting vehemence. In any case it reveals the unconscious desire to draw attention, to warn, to shock, to show the red light. Few people regularly use red ink in writing, but many would avoid it at any price. Of two handwritings written in red ink which have impressed me in recent years, one was produced by a boy who at the age of thirteen killed another boy from jealousy; the second was a signature by George Bernard Shaw. The unhappy boy, with his passionate tension, on the one hand, the accusing, revolutionary critic and censor of our social institutions, who wished to shock the *bourgeois*, on the other, are two extremes which both chose the colour red.

The colour violet, the colour of Buddha and Buddhism, contains an element of mystery, of Eastern dreams, of kindliness. It was for a time also the fashionable colour, and early graphology interpreted it as a passion for the fashionable.

Green, the colour of Mahomet, is in popular belief the colour of hope, in the occult the colour of folly. It is the colour of grass and woods, of summer and spring. In medicine it is the colour of relief and recovery for tired eyes. Early graphology interpreted it as a desire to be a bit apart and out of the ordinary.

Blue, the colour of the Virgin, the mystical colour of virtue and regeneration, the colour of the sky and of the sea, has to be divided into dark blue and light blue. Light blue, the water-colour type, reflects the sky-blue and rather watery and conventional dreams of girlhood, the Hollywood approach.

Black, in all shades, and blue-black, are the conventional colours of writing; and here only the shading is of major interest. But a very dark, intense black writing mostly conveys a tendency to sensuality, as well as to depression.

Before we start analysing shading of the stroke, it may here be repeated that the use of inks of different colours in the same writing (two or more) reveals the shock-stricken, isolated mind of the lunatic.

While the study of colours has not progressed far yet and is, apart from exceptional cases, of comparatively minor importance, the character and shading of the stroke itself has, in the last fifteen years, been to the fore of continental research work. Such able investigators as Frau Dr. M. Hartge, the late Reader in Graphology at Freiburg University, Dr. R. Prophal, Professor of Graphology at Hamburg University, Frau Dr. Roda Wieser, outstanding Austrian graphologist and former assistant of the Institute of Criminology of Vienna University, and Walter Hegar, German-born, now French graphologist, are and have been devoted to this work. In addition, the studies of the Dutch graphologist, H. Brail, on the character of the stroke of insane persons, may be recorded.

Let us start with Brail's findings. A thorough investigation of a number of writings of mentally sick persons, and especially of schizophrenics, has shown that while the great majority of lunatics show a very thin, colourless stroke, the writing of the schizophrenics, in a great number of cases, shows striking and sudden changes from thin, colourless to extremely thick strokes of a colourful shock character.

It should be remembered that the character of the stroke is produced by different elements:

(*a*) by the wish of the writer to produce just the impression which this particular stroke creates, according to his guiding image; and

(*b*) by the motor impulses—his grip, sense of touch and time— which enable him to carry out the appropriate pressure and movement.

This second element belongs, of course, to dynamics, to the kinaesthetic side of graphology and is, therefore, outside the scope of this book, which deals with the guiding image only. What is said here covers only a part of the problem which is now in the forefront of research work. Graphology more and more realizes that the basic rhythm, the coherence and integration of the stroke, is an indicator of the general standard of a person's participation in life, colouring and grading his chance of realizing his guiding images, his basic conceptions.

It was a study of the writings of major criminals undertaken by Frau Dr. Hartge at the instigation of the graphologist and neuro-logist, Dr. Muthmann, which started this line of research, and it was on the writing of criminals that Professor Pophal based his book *Das Strichbild*, and that Frau Dr. Roda Wieser in her standard work *The Criminal and His Handwriting* came to her conclusions.

I myself, to check up on these results, undertook an investigation into the writing of fifty highly intelligent (according to their I.Q.) juvenile delinquents and compared them with the writing of picked reliable boys of the same age group. I found that 46 per cent of the delinquents as against o per cent of the good boys had a noticeably lifeless stroke, and that 70 per cent of the good boys as against only 16 per cent of the delinquents had a noticeably lively stroke. The rest were not striking in either of these directions.

An investigation not only of the liveliness, but of the whole rhythmic character of the stroke and of the manuscript gave even more definite results. Grading the rhythm of the writing into five degrees—the first two representing good rhythm, the last two very poor rhythm—the distribution was as follows:

Rhythm 2: 70 per cent of the good boys as against 4 per cent of the delinquents.

Rhythm 3: 30 per cent of the good boys as against 58 per cent of the delinquents.

Rhythm 4: 32 per cent of the delinquents, none of the good boys.

Rhythm 5: 6 per cent of the delinquents, none of the good boys.

The portrayal of the different degrees of liveliness or lifelessness of the strokes in books suffers from alterations of colour and character of the stroke through the reproduction process necessary for printing. It may, however, be said that the lively stroke is firm, well framed and, at the same time, shaded, showing a rhythmic integration of slightly lighter and slightly stronger pressure, corresponding to a rhythmic ebb and flow of effort and relaxation. Example 168 may best explain this type of stroke.

Among the lifeless strokes we have, according to the above-mentioned research works, to make a subdivision between the monotonous dead stroke, Example 169 (Pophal calls it amorphous), and the weak disintegrating stroke, Example 170 (Pophal calls it granulated).

EXAMPLE 168
The lively stroke

EXAMPLE 169
The monotonous dead stroke

EXAMPLE 170
The disintegrating stroke

The first shows no ebb and flow, but a constant degree of effort without relaxation, a flat approach to life; while the latter shows a looseness which does not allow for any real effort. The interpretation of these different degrees of liveliness of the stroke is obvious: the lively stroke reveals a healthy and harmonious participation in life, the ability to adjust oneself to its basic rhythm. As such it is an indicator of a high probability of adjustment of personal conceptions to the demands of life.

The monotonous stroke is an indicator of a condition of dull unrelaxed tension, with the emotional and sentimental life blunted, and sympathy and adaptation blocked.

The disintegrating stroke reveals an incapacity for harmonious effort, for constructive form and production, and an inability to realize and put into effect one's own ideas.

It is, therefore, the case that while the rhythmical, shaded, lively stroke is a positive index of the writer's guiding image, pointing to reliability and achievement, the lifeless or unrhythmically shaded, or flat, unshaded stroke is a negative index, almost always present in the writing of people who have failed to realize their guiding images in their actual life.

CHAPTER XVIII

THE HARD CORE OF THE HANDWRITING

AT the end of this study of the guiding image in handwriting I feel that the reader may be slightly confused. "If", he may argue, "the constant relation between individual handwriting and individual personality is the basis of graphological assessment, the great number of different factors mentioned (the difference between official and unofficial personality, the influences of evocative words and associations, the suggestions emanating from the person of the addressee or other names, the impact of environment, situations and changes on an individual manuscript) may confuse the issue to a degree that a reliable assessment may become impossible."

For that reason I consider it worth while, legitimate and necessary to finish this book with a chapter which clearly sets out to define to what degree the basic image of the writer, his coordinating *Gestalt*-principle, can be affected by the factors mentioned, and to what extent the hard core of his personality and the hard core of his writing image will resist any outside influence.

To do this it is advisable to treat implications caused by moods and distractions differently from those caused by suggestive words and names, and, finally, differently from those caused by discrepancy between official and unofficial personality.

Real changes in the guiding conceptions of human beings have been discussed in chapter XVI, and do not, of course, come into the scope of this chapter.

The investigation may be started with a reassurance. None of the influences mentioned in this chapter and the corresponding changes in writing affect the basic core of the personal make-up. Not only have numerous experiments in writing with different limbs, right and left hand, toes, etc., proved that normally a writer's guiding image never changes, but even a change of writing styles does not affect the basic formula of proportions, as the very interesting investigation of the American Professor Werner Wolff has shown. He found that—as each personality needs a certain regularity of proportion for its own security's sake—every signature which he investigated contained in itself a unit of length for measurement, of which the single parts of the whole signature were only proportionate multiples. .

As a second consideration, the fact that a man behaves differently in his public life from his private, that he is affected by suggestions implied in words, names and associations, or prone to moods and distractions of his environment, is in itself an important influence on his character. What may be, however, questioned is whether it is always possible to discern and to separate the writing and personality trends which are constant from those which are casually caused by one of the reasons mentioned.

Although it requires great experience, and although it is desirable to have more than one specimen of writing to be able to separate these trends, it is of course possible, and there are clear-cut rules for doing it. Even if there is only one manuscript available it may be possible to say which parts of it look affected by casual influences or artificial behaviour and which do not.

Let us take the three groups of influences separately.

(*a*) Stimulating words or associations, imitative suggestions. It is easy to see that the stimulations or inhibitions radiating from a single word or a single association will affect only the writing of this individual word and will leave the rest of the writing intact.

Strong imitative impulses, which go so far as to make the writer imitate the writing of the addressee, are extremely rare; but even so, they affect only certain elements, which are elaborated in the paragraph on artificial writing. If two manuscripts of the writer are available, one of which is not written to the same addressee as the other, a comparison easily shows what they have in common and what is superimposed.

(*b*) The influence of moods and environments. Influences on handwriting originating from moods will affect only the extension and direction of the writing. As in the writing of people suffering from psychic diseases, the depressive moods will make the writing smaller and narrower and will make the line sag down, while pleasure and excitement will make the writing bigger and broader, and the line will rise.

States of high-pitched tension or exhaustion will, in addition, reflect on the pressure and the firmness of the stroke, also the straightness of the line. States of disease or alcoholic intoxication fall into the same category.

Shocks of any kind will affect the continuity of the stroke and cause breaks.

The forms and proportions of letters, the general layout, the basic rhythm, will never be substantially affected.

(c) Official (artificial) and natural (spontaneous) writing. The rules set out here apply also in a still wider sense to disguised writing. Where material for comparison is available, or where only part is official writing and the other part natural, the artificial parts will always be the ones where the writing elements producible by will and control are more frequent. Any kind of artificial and stylized writing will also allow for distinction between the deeper layer of the suppressed natural image of the writer and the superimposed image of his hetero-ego, of his official self.

It is Ludwig Klages whom, as for so many other things, we have to thank for the clearest system for distinguishing these two layers. There are two basic rules, of which the first has been already mentioned. Everything which can be produced by will can more easily be artificially added, while any attempt to loosen the writing artificially produces considerable difficulties, if it has to be constantly applied at natural speed.

The elements which are characteristic of will and control are smallness, narrowness, extension downwards, disconnection, regularity, upright and left slant, complications, angular and copybook connections, block letters. The elements which are characteristic of ease and looseness, and therefore difficult to produce, are breadth, proportion, connectedness, garland- and thread-writing, upper length extension, irregularity, bad layout, simplification, cursive writing.

The second rule deals with the degree of attention. Everything in the limelight—ego-symbols, address, capitals and beginnings of words, down-strokes—will be more easily altered than small letters, *i*-dots, ends of words, connecting strokes. For this reason people with a loose, easy handwriting are better forgers and cleverer in disguising their writing than people whose handwriting is consistently subjected to will and control, as I have been able to convince myself in many cases of poison-pen letters and disguised writing.

BIBLIOGRAPHY

WRITTEN IN GERMAN

Ludwig Klages: *Handschrift und Charakter*. Ambrosius Barth, Muenchen.

Max Pulver: *Symbolik der Handschrift*. Orell Fuessli, Zurich.

Carl Gross: *Vitalitaet und Handschrift*. Ludwig Rohrscheid, Bonn.

Rudolph Pophal: *Das Strichbild*. Georg Thieme, Stuttgart. *Die Handschrift als Gehirnschrift*. Greifen Verlag, Rudolstadt.

Rudolphine Poppee: *Graphologie*. E. E. Weber, Leipzig.

Roda Wieser: *Der Verbrecher und seine Handschrift*. Altdorfer Verlag, Stuttgart.

Hans Knobloch: *Die Lebensgestalt der Handschrift*. West-Ost Verlag, Saarbruecken.

Magda Hartge: "Bericht ueber das Ergebnis einer Untersuchung der Handschriften von 28 Schwerverbrechern." Article in *Zentralblatt fuer Graphologie*. "Die Schriftspannung." Article in *Die Schrift*.

M. A. Brail: *Graphologische Untersuchungen ueber die Psychomotorik in Handschriften Schizophrener*. S. Karger, New York und Basel.

Wilfred Daim: *Handschrift und Existenz*. Anton Pustet, Graz.

Eric Singer: *Die Handschrift sagt Alles*. Paul List, Muenchen.

H. Rohrschach: *Diagnostik*, Bern.

Siegmund Freud: *Vorlesungen zur Einfuehrung in die Psychoanalyse*. Internat. Psychoanalytischer Verlag, Wien.

E. Bleuler: *Lehrbuch der Psychiatrie*. Julius Springer, Berlin.

WRITTEN IN FRENCH

E. De Rougement: *La Graphologie*. Marcel Rivière, Paris.

Anja Teillard: *L'âme et l'écriture*. Stock, Paris.

J. Crépieu-Jamin: *Les bases fondamentales de la Graphologie et de l'expertise en Ecriture*. Alcan, Paris. *L'écriture et le Caractère*. Presses Universtaires de France, Paris. *Les Eléments de l'écriture de Canailles*. Flammarion, Paris.

Eric Singer—Cyrille de Neubourg: "Petit précis de la graphologie practique." Magazine *Elle*, Paris.

Devoilè: "Les Mystères des Couleurs." Magazine *Elle*, Paris.

WRITTEN IN ENGLISH

Werner Wolff: *Diagrams of the Unconscious*. Grune & Stratton, New York.

Robert Saudek: *Experiments with Handwriting*. Allen & Unwin, London. *What your Handwriting Shows*. Werner Laurie, London.

Olga Marum. *Character Assessment from Handwriting*. Bartholomew Press, Dorking.